LISTENING

━━━ WITH ━━━

EMPATHY

Also by John Selby

Take Charge of Your Mind

LISTENING
— WITH —
EMPATHY

Creating Genuine Connections with
Customers and Colleagues

John SELBY

HAMPTON ROADS
PUBLISHING COMPANY, INC.

Cover design by Frame25 Productions
Cover art by Gautier Willaume, c/o Shutterstock

Hampton Roads Publishing Company, Inc.
1125 Stoney Ridge Road
Charlottesville, VA 22902

434-296-2772
fax: 434-296-5096
e-mail: hrpc@hrpub.com
www.hrpub.com

If you are unable to order this book from your local
bookseller, you may order directly from the publisher.
Call 1-800-766-8009, toll-free.

Library of Congress Cataloging-in-Publication Data

Selby, John, 1945-
  Listening with empathy : creating genuine connections with customers and
colleagues / John Selby.
      p. cm.
  Summary: "John Selby presents his four-step Listening with Empathy mood-
management method for rapidly shifting from negative to positive moods at work,
feeling good in your own skin in the present moment, and making authentic heart
contact with customers, clients, and colleagues"--Provided by publisher.
  ISBN 1-57174-514-9 (5 x 7 tc : alk. paper)
  1. Success in business--Psychological aspects. 2. Listening--Psychological
aspects. 3. Empathy. I. Title.
  HF5386.S4168 2007
  650.1--dc22

                    2006033709

ISBN 1-57174-514-9
10 9 8 7 6 5 4 3 2 1
Printed on acid-free paper in China

THE DILEMMA . . . AND ITS RESOLUTION

We're all being pressured at work to create and sustain genuine, emotional engagement and long-term loyalty with clients and co-workers. No matter how good our product or service, or how sharp our intellect, if we can't regularly make meaningful heart contact and maintain a bright, empathic presence at work, our prosperity will suffer. Therefore, we need to know how to shift quickly from dull, negative moods into bright, cheerful emotions – so that we can listen with empathy, respond with compassion, and generate trust.

No one wants to do business with someone who's not fully present and honestly attentive. Customers, clients, and co-workers need to feel genuinely heard, accepted, and appreciated – and this means your emotions and actions must be consistently genuine rather than put-on.

The good news in this regard is that you naturally possess the ability to take charge of your moods, to shift rapidly from negative to positive emotions, and to listen with heartfelt presence.

The four-phase Listening with Empathy mood-management program taught in this book is a trustworthy inner method that you can use at work to put aside inappropriate moods, activate your empathy power, and relate with genuine consideration. Here's our logic: When you feel good inside your own skin, you naturally interact with honest, bright emotions. The trick is in learning how to shift quickly into an enjoyable mood at work so that you listen with empathy, make genuine heart contact – and enjoy each new encounter as you become more confident, charismatic, and successful.

Feel Better Inside ➡ Listen with Empathy ➡ Enjoy Your Success

LISTENING WITH EMPATHY: THE METHOD

Traditional psychological approaches for improving customer experience employed mostly techniques that tried to manipulate customer emotions. Our new approach is participatory rather than manipulative – teaching you how to shift inwardly from negative to positive moods, and thus become genuinely friendly and helpful. Our Listening with Empathy method will enable you to move through the following four customer-encounter phases with high success:

Phase 1 – Preparation: Before meeting with a customer or client, it's vital to put aside any stress, worries, or judgments that may pollute the encounter – and shift your focus toward positive feelings and heart-centered emotions.

Phase 2 – The Moment of Encounter: Right when you meet someone, you need to present an honest, friendly, nonjudgmental greeting, and offer relaxed space. New techniques can help you maintain a bright inner center, emit a friendly presence, and converse with relaxed spontaneity, acceptance, and enjoyment.

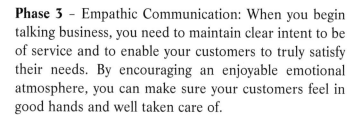

Phase 3 – Empathic Communication: When you begin talking business, you need to maintain clear intent to be of service and to enable your customers to truly satisfy their needs. By encouraging an enjoyable emotional atmosphere, you can make sure your customers feel in good hands and well taken care of.

Phase 4 – Processing: This fourth phase involves pausing after a meeting to reflect on a recent sales or service encounter and to decide purposefully how to follow up on it. You'll learn to re-experience positive aspects of the encounter and focus on your desire to meet with this customer again.

RAPID LEARNING CURVE

You'll be surprised at how quickly you can learn to take charge of your moods and attitudes and to shift at will into more friendly, accepting, engaging emotions both at work and in your private life. You already have the power to make such a shift – this method provides the special tools that enable you to activate your power so you can shift on demand into more positive thoughts and moods.

This mood-shifting process will make you feel immediately better so that you'll naturally begin using these tools right away, applying them regularly in all aspects of your life.

Please don't think here in the beginning that you're being judged as in any way inadequate with your present emotional performance at work. Such self-judgment is entirely unproductive. What's important is accepting and honoring yourself just as you are, and then learning how to optimize your natural warmth and personal presence in sales and service situations.

The discussions and programs in this book will teach you all you need to know for activating the Listening with Empathy program at work. For those of you who value audio guidance for learning a method, we also offer full online support at www.listeningwithempathy.com. There you'll find a full set of emotional-recovery and relationship-improvement courses to help you further master your moods and brighten your attitudes toward life.

I welcome you to this new emotional-boosting method. Take time to learn the process by heart, use the online audio training support also if you like, and for the rest of your life, actively employ your inner power to shift away from negative moods to your natural brightness and a successful presence at work!

TABLE OF CONTENTS

PHASE FOUR: POST-ENCOUNTER PROCESSING

QUICK FIND PAGE – PRIMARY EXERCISES

INTRODUCTION

EMOTIONAL ENGAGEMENT IN THE WORKPLACE

The greatest challenge currently facing companies, especially sales and service companies, is learning how to establish genuine emotional involvement with each new customer or client. This is equally true with co-workers at all levels – building lasting personal relationships is the human foundation upon which all companies survive. Employee empathy and the resulting customer or client satisfaction and loyalty are the buzzwords of sustainable success.

In this book, I'd like to teach you an advanced program that targets the four key flashpoints of successful emotional engagement at work. Through a special application of cognitive science, mind-heart integration research, and a good dose of common sense, this new empathy-boosting method will ensure an enhancement of trust and loyalty in your sales and service activities, your involvement with colleagues, and also your interactions with friends and family.

Although the method you are about to learn appears quite short, simple, and easy to learn, the underlying psychological theory and process are quite complex and have taken more than 30 years to develop.

I began my professional career doing mind and mood research at the National Institute of Mental Health (NIMH) and other formal institutions, and then I spent many years in private practice exploring the relationship between the thoughts we habitually hold in our minds and the moods we experience as a result. Over the last decade, I've researched corporate applications of my work, applied my discoveries to specific workplace dilemmas, and developed online training and executive coaching formats to make the new methods available to all.

The truth is that we live in a society that spends 15 to 20 years training its youngsters intellectually to perform well at work, but devotes almost no training to emotive dimensions of relating and success.

Hopefully, methods such as the one in this book will quickly get us up to speed regarding the basics of consciousness management and successful relating on all fronts because developing our latent potential for listening with empathy and generating lasting relationships, both at work and in our private lives, is vital to our personal well-being – and to the well-being of our companies.

Luckily, most of what I'm going to teach you is relatively easy to grasp because it rings true with common sense. Even though some of the psychological concepts you'll be learning in this book may be new, you'll know from experience that we're describing how you run emotionally – and you'll be able to readily apply the new methods to your daily lives. You'll also find that each step of this process is a pleasure – because you're learning how to enjoy yourself more at work.

GENUINE EMOTIONAL ENGAGEMENT

A recent study documents that more than two-thirds of all customers consider their emotional experience in the store or office in which they work the most important factor in their choice of whether to return to that particular enterprise. Positive customer experience is the edge that brings customers back for more business. The same is true in any type of client relationship. But what actually constitutes a *positive customer experience*, and how can this experience be genuinely stimulated?

In most companies, much valuable effort has already been exerted to create an environmental atmosphere that pleases customers and makes them want to return. And, certainly, most do their best to provide goods and services that are of high quality.

The key missing variable in the customer experience equation deals specifically with that more subtle aspect of the customer experience – the emotional impact of the employee upon a customer's experience and empathic needs.

For various outmoded reasons, traditional psychological approaches to improving customer/client engagement and loyalty have been based on theories that try to take advantage of customer gullibility to evoke a positive emotional experience. In this scenario, the employee is trained to manipulate the emotions of the customer in desired directions.

Unfortunately, this situation very often backfires. There's nothing more bothersome to a customer than walking into a store and being lambasted by phony employee grins and ego-boosting comments. Yes, such manipulations might work once – but they too often eliminate customer loyalty and future sales.

The Listening with Empathy approach for generating a positive customer/client experience goes entirely beyond the idea of covertly training employee behavior. Dropping down to a deeper level of relationship dynamics, this approach builds on the core ingredients of all successful long-term relationships: emotional honesty, spontaneous genuine interaction, and a sincere interest in the well-being of another.

Customers are sensitive creatures, and you are the primary, active ingredient that determines the experience they will have in your business. Their inner experiences are responses to your inner experience. Therefore, customer experience is determined primarily by employee mood and behavior.

In this introduction, we will quickly review the basic mind-management method taught in my book, *Take Charge of Your Mind: Core Skills to Enhance Your Performance, Well-Being, and Integrity at Work*, which lays the foundation for managing your moods at work. We'll then advance into new empathy-boosting techniques that enable you to broadcast a positive presence that becomes the key ingredient of your customers' experiences.

Being genuine with your emotions is absolutely required in this customer-first approach. But, we all sometimes have difficulty being friendly; we're all packing our fair share of shyness, inhibitions, hurt feelings, and under-pressure aggressions and resentments.

What I want to teach you in this book is how to manage negative emotional moods so that you have a conscious choice concerning which mood or emotion you broadcast at work. Rather than being a victim of your moods, you can become master of them.

FOUR KEY ENCOUNTER PHASES

Each time you prepare for and enter into an encounter with a customer, client, colleague, or friend, you actually move through four phases of the basic interactive experience. In this book, we'll examine these phases in depth and discover exactly what you can do in each to optimize success. Let's look a step more deeply into these four phases here, and then spend the rest of the book mastering each phase.

Phase 1: Preparation

Almost always before you move into a face-to-face or telephone encounter with someone, you have at least a few moments, perhaps a minute or two, to prepare. My method will enable you to pause and quickly examine your prevailing thoughts, mood, and energetic condition, and to shift out of negative states into positive states rapidly – before you enter (and alter) the emotional environment of the other person.

We all have both positive and negative emotions that we can focus on every moment. This new technique is all about learning how to shift your conscious focus toward your heart and to awaken your more positive emotions.

> This first phase of the Listening with Empathy process involves the crucial act of taking time to consciously choose your mood – rather than just blundering into an encounter and running on automatic.

Please note that in this program you're not being asked to permanently repress your negative feelings. If you have deeper emotional issues that need attention beyond the scope of this book, you'll find further assistance at this level at my online support center. General emotional expression and health are vital. But, what we're focusing on here is your power to master your moods specifically at work so that you present appropriate emotions on the job – and stop sabotaging your success.

Phase 2: The Moment of Encounter

All too often, people tend to go momentarily unconscious when first meeting someone, slipping into old habits and patterns that are less than optimal. The second section of this book explores this crucial moment of encounter. Through dramatic real-world examples, you'll see how varying attitudes provoke quite different responses in customers. Right at the moment of encounter, you can choose the attitude of expressing an honest, friendly, nonjudgmental greeting. You can also offer a relaxed emotional breathing space for the person you're meeting.

> As you broadcast an expanded quality of positive consciousness, you'll encourage the person you're with to also feel good, relaxed, and accepted.

The primary skill you learn to master in this phase is your often dormant ability to simply enjoy the present moment, interact spontaneously, and broadcast heartfelt, empathic emotions. This skill can be readily learned once the psychological process is understood and experienced as a clear, cognitive process.

In this discussion, we'll look honestly – with acceptance and understanding – at your inherited attitudes and habitual moods. Step by step, we'll develop your ability to keep positive feelings dominant at work. We'll also explore your ability to shift out of fear-based aggressive feelings into an emotional state where you fully accept the person you're with and enjoy sharing space with them.

Phase 3: Empathic Communication

At some point, small talk ends and sales talk or active service begins. Too often, this is when a customer or client suddenly feels his or her enjoyment of the moment collapse – when the sales person shifts into manipulative thoughts, emotions, and behavior. I would like to teach you how to avoid slipping into traditional sales push mentality so that you maintain a clear intent to be of service to your customer.

Here's the reality: Customers bond with company representatives only when they experience a heart connection that feels genuinely good, trustworthy, and enjoyable.

In this context, the shift from preliminary chat into serious business action does not need to lose this heart connection, nor the feeling of mutual trust. Through several examples, we'll see in action how your inner choices in this regard determine the quality of the customer's experience.

Most pressured sales pitches are ultimately fear based – the sales person is anxious about losing a sale and cleverly pushes to force one. In the new customer-centered marketplace, such fear-based manipulation is a serious negative because most customers don't like feeling pressured and dominated – and won't return. Instead, we'll explore the customer's desire to express his or her need and your responsibility to meet that need.

In the midst of such genuine emotional engagement, trust is generated – and lasting bonds are established. When the customer is allowed full freedom of choice in a sales decision, and helped to make the decision that is right for her/him, customer loyalty soars. As a spin-off benefit, you'll feel good for having truly been of service – and because you feel good, you'll also succeed with your next customer or client.

Phase 4: Processing

Many people think a sales or service encounter is over when the customer leaves. However, there is a vital fourth phase to any successful encounter – where you spend essential moments reflecting on the encounter, and then deciding how best to follow up.

As you'll learn step by step, during this fourth phase you can purposefully pause and fortify your intent to continue to hold this person regularly in your mind. You can re-experience positive aspects of the encounter and focus on your desire to meet with this person again. During this fourth phase, you can advance short-term into long-term memory and consciously establish a lasting sense of connection with the person.

Mastering the ability to successfully let go of negative judgments and accept customers just as they are is central to success with this method – because the thoughts you think about a person do actually impact that person.

Based on the impressive Princeton Engineering Anomalies

Research (PEAR) program, there is now scientific evidence proving that the thoughts you think about someone can actually influence that person's impressions and emotions – even from a distance. This might sound like science fiction, but the evidence of the PEAR studies and related research has proven that our minds do broadcast information and intent that other people can receive at a distance (see www.princeton.edu/~pear).

This new research demonstrates that before, during, and after a business encounter, as a company representative, you need to maintain an accepting, positive attitude toward the customer. Otherwise, your negative thoughts and emotions will influence and pollute the customer experience. Conversely, when you pause to think with welcome emotions about a customer, you're actively encouraging that client or customer to return.

PSYCHOLOGY OF EXPERIENCE

The business world has now reached a remarkable tipping point, as executives begin to realize that doing business is as much about experience as it is about product. In so many industries, more and more corporations offer basically the same product or service; therefore, in order to flourish into the future, companies more and more realize that they must do more than pay lip service to mastering the key intangible sales variable – customer experience.

The term "customer experience" is much bandied about these days, but mostly at shallow levels. In this book, I want to take you to the heart of what "customer experience" is all about. We need to see, quite logically and from a psychological point of view, how customer experience is very much determined by . . . employee experience.

> Logic dictates that when an employee feels genuinely good, the customer responds positively. But when an employee feels bad or depressed, angry or bored, judgmental or otherwise negative, the customer gets hit with this negative emotional atmosphere – and won't want to return.

This is why alert employers are now becoming more and more hyper-concerned about the prevailing moods and attitudes of their employees. Traditionally, employers felt they had no need and, indeed, perhaps no right to interfere with the inner emotional experience of an employee. As with religious freedom of expression, employees were mostly granted the right to their own feelings – as long as those feelings didn't interfere with their work. However, we've now entered a period of history where an employee's inner experience is clearly identified as either interfering with or aiding in all customer-related activities.

Throughout this book I would like to explore with you the ethics behind this new dilemma, where companies want to insist that employees manage their minds and emotions according to employer dictates – or get fired. Is this fair? As you'll see, the basic mind-management and mood-management methods taught in this book are designed to nurture the well-being and freedom of the employee. They are not in any way to be used as forced manipulative tools.

In each section of this book you'll see how an employee's inner experience must be honored and supported, but never manipulated. Why? Because only when an employee feels free will that employee express positive emotions, which customers want and will return for in order to share again. This is the beautiful built-in "employee freedom" clause in my method: It only works when it's used to set employees free to feel good; not in any way to fake feeling good.

Many companies are still employing manipulative methods to engineer customer experience by trying to engineer employee behavior. But, as we'll see in this discussion, cheating our emotions seldom works. Usually the heart knows when it's being manipulated. Most customers can sense when employee emotions aren't genuine, and because customers are now king and queen, manipulative methods to provoke customer bonding simply won't work in the long run. However, fair methods that honestly encourage good feelings in the hearts of employees *will* work. This book is all about supporting this basic employee right to feel good while at work.

We've reached a positive period in business history where employers must guarantee employees the right to enjoy their work – otherwise, customers will react negatively and not engage with that enterprise.

In this new spirit of helping the workplace become a more enjoyable place in which to spend a third of your life, I welcome you to explore this book and its new process for learning how to truly have a good time on the job – and for succeeding because you're having a good time.

MIND/HEART INTEGRATION

In the old days, we were all supposed to leave our heartfelt emotions and spontaneity at the door – along with our religion and politics – when we entered the workplace because, supposedly, there was no room for personal emotions on the job. The less engaged you were with your emotions and deeper intuitive self, the better (it was assumed) you would perform at work.

Actually, that old stereotype of a hard-hearted corporate chief and tough-minded, heartless employees was never fully adhered to at work. Sometimes the more aggressive, heartless guy in the gang would rise to the top on the backs of everybody else. But, even traditionally, team spirit and a sense of company heart and soul have been the foundation of American business. So it's no new discovery that truly friendly, service-oriented sales people often outsell the manipulators. I'm not the first to bring heart into the business scenario.

What's happening, finally, is the open acknowledgment throughout the business world that heart and soul, intuition, spiritual integrity, and deeper wisdom do have essential roles to play in the pragmatic process of winning in business.

The challenge is how to consciously encourage these qualities at work – because they cannot be manipulated into existence. Rather, they come into being when certain positive emotional and mental conditions are nurtured in the workplace. In *Take Charge of Your Mind,* I address these underlying issues in short form. In this new book, we have the opportunity to look deeper into the actual psychological dynamics of bringing more heart into the work experience.

With customer-first imperatives now ruling the situation, we're not only free to talk about the integration of mind and heart – we urgently need to address this crucial issue, and act on it.

STAYING GENUINE IN DIFFICULT SITUATIONS

There are two quite different aspects of this method. First of all, yes, we do need to learn specific inner techniques that enable us to manage our own emotions and maintain a genuinely bright and friendly presence at work. But, we also need to learn how to successfully deal with customers who bang at us with negative moods and agendas. All too often our customers and clients manage to push our buttons and provoke a reaction inside us that further undermines the emotional atmosphere of the moment. We all know what it feels like to get hit in our emotional gut by an angry customer, dragged down by a depressed client, or agitated by an anxious co-worker.

> How can you master the fine art of making sure you help raise your customers emotionally rather than being dragged down by them? In each of the four Listening with Empathy phases you'll learn how to prepare yourself for a negative customer or client and how to deal with this negativity in a positive way.

There's a curious psychological twist to this aspect of sales and service. Very often your most loyal customers are those who first entered your business or store feeling low and down, and then found their spirits rising through their interactions with you. If you can succeed in raising the spirits of your customers, they will be especially thankful and want to return often.

So, throughout this book you'll learn specific tricks and methods for holding your own against the down pull of customers caught in their own negative inner dramas. I'll show you emotional muscle-building exercises that, over time, will help you develop more and more inner strength to withstand the gale of negative moods customers bring into your stores and offices. If you learn not to react, but rather to accept the mood of a customer, you then give this person space to recover and feel better. This is the gift a friend gives a friend, after all. It's time to apply the "best friend" psychological logic to the workplace.

PRACTICAL ACTION

Overall, this is an action book. Based on the following four indicators, the scene is set for you to master the Listening with Empathy method.

1. The business logic is clear: With customer loyalty the most valued commodity in the workplace, we must actively develop our natural human capacity to bond emotionally with each new customer and, through honest service and friendship, establish customer relationships that endure and expand.

2. The method is here: In this book, you will learn psychological processes that enable you to identify your emotional choices and to shift your focus in directions that nurture good feelings. You'll learn how to accomplish this emotional-shifting process right in the heat of your work life. Furthermore, you'll learn ways to integrate your mind and your heart so that you're experienced as a whole person at work – and, therefore, able to genuinely make friends and be of service to your customers.

3. The delivery system is in place: Through reading this book and practicing its four-step method, you'll receive full instruction for mastering the mind-heart integration challenge. If you want audio guidance in learning the process, I also offer online support and training to augment this written guidance.

4. Motivation is high: We all want success at work. In addition, we want to enjoy our lives while on the job and to feel that we're truly being of service in the world. The method taught in this book is easy to learn. You'll enjoy each day of training – and, as you apply what you've learned, you'll find that you continue to get better and better at customer bonding and sales.

So, enjoy this book. Learn how to set yourself free at work. And, as you set yourself free and tap more genuine emotional expression, you'll watch your success rise as your feelings soar!

Preparing for an Encounter

CHAPTER 1

SHIFT FROM HEAD TO HEART

Early in his career, George demonstrated a "sales charm" presence that his colleagues in his chosen field of health insurance envied. He was naturally charismatic, dominant, confident, and successful. He could gracefully, but forcefully, overpower a potential client and push most sales through. But, with the changing marketplace and more emphasis on genuine customer experience and long-term satisfaction, George found that he was closing fewer sales and also losing customer loyalty and renewals. Something in his sales routine wasn't working anymore.

His company began distributing short customer satisfaction surveys to its clients and George received numerous complaints. Customers wouldn't tell him to his face that they found him pushy and insincere, but they didn't respond positively to his overbearing tactics for closing a sale and they preferred to get their insurance elsewhere next time or have a different company rep visit them.

Hearing the results of this report, George was at a total loss. His old manipulative sales routine wasn't working anymore – but he had no idea what he could do to be more genuinely friendly. Like so many people, he felt a prisoner of his own moods and conditioning. When I first began working with him, one-on-one in private training, he felt offended, depressed, and hopeless – and angry for being harshly judged. His dad had been a great old-time salesman and George had just inherited the family routines.

In our first couple of sessions, he felt hurt and he floundered in defensive emotions. But, then George began to realize that the situation was not as bad as he thought. He learned that certain effective techniques could empower him to wake up his sales career, and to feel more genuinely friendly and positive in the bargain. Thus encouraged, he quickly shifted into action and went to work mastering the basic process. After three weeks of training, George was discovering that by giving himself permission to relax and feel genuinely good in the present moment, he could relate with clients without being pushy. Step by step he found a new confidence based on a sense of helpful participation in clients' lives. He also found that his ability to relate to his wife and two boys improved.

As George unleashed his inherent ability to come more from the heart and be honest with his emotions, he realized that his real sales power wasn't grounded in selfishly manipulating people, but in working with them to identify their needs and to do what he could to satisfy them.

In general, learning to be consistently positive and genuinely supportive in our lives means consciously shifting our focus of attention away from manipulating the world and toward more fully participating in each new moment. This is what empathy training is all about. In this first chapter, I'd like to teach you the first step I taught George – how to consciously manage your thoughts and moods before you enter into a sales, service, or teamwork situation so that you can make more contact with your feelings and awaken your empathic powers.

All you need are the basic cognitive tools for making this shift and, of course, some daily practice. I'll teach you the process, and then you provide the practice – through ten minutes of dedicated learning each day for the next few weeks. Is that a reasonable arrangement? You'll also find an audio online support program at our Listening with Empathy website to guide you through a daily empathy fitness program. Even in the first week of working with this method, you'll experience positive results. As a valuable bonus, you'll find that as you master this process your entire life will become brighter, friendlier, and more successful.

DEFINING EMPATHY

The business community has used the word "empathy" somewhat loosely. What is actually meant by the word? From the dictionary, we see that empathy comes from the Greek noun *empatheia,* meaning passion, or *empathes,* emotional. The formal definition states that empathy is the action of understanding, being aware of, being sensitive to, and vicariously experiencing the feelings, thoughts, and experience of another.

Notice that empathy isn't just an idea; it's an action – in which you experience another person's presence and feelings in your own emotional system, stimulated by your present-moment awareness of another person's thoughts, moods, and actions.

In other words, rather than staying overly fixated on your own feelings and thoughts when you meet someone, to feel empathy you need to shift your focus of attention strongly toward the physical presence and experience of the other person.

This means that, if you want to express empathy when you meet someone, you should probably prepare yourself beforehand so that you're in the proper state of mind to be aware and sensitive, and able to experience what the person you're meeting is feeling at the moment. If you're naturally in peak empathic condition in the moment, then no preparation is needed – but most of us most are usually in the opposite state.

We're focused on our own thoughts and emotions, rather than the thoughts and emotions of others.

Let's also look at what it really means to be "friendly" since this term is often used interchangeably with empathic. The dictionary tells us that being friendly means showing kindly interest and goodwill; being cheerful, comforting, and helpful. Again we see the clear intent – to perceive the need of another person and to express positive, cheerful concern for that person's well-being. Being friendly also means being of service and help to another person.

Especially in the realm of sales and service work, the words "friendly," "empathic," and the phrase "ready to serve" reflect the basic state of awareness that will make customers and clients feel accepted, understood, and well taken care of. "We offer friendly service" is the general motto of every successful business – but the vital question remains: How can you make sure before you enter into a service situation that you are in the right state of mind and mood to be genuinely helpful and friendly?

FOUR EMPATHY VARIABLES

From a psychological perspective, there are four primary variables that determine whether you are warm and friendly, or just the opposite. You'll notice that each of the following inner variables relates to how you manage your own moment-to-moment focus of attention. Your power of attention is, indeed, as I point out in many of my books, the underlying mental tool at your immediate disposal to take charge of your inner power and direct it where you want it.

When you focus your attention in certain directions (on the past or the future, on negative memories, on your own concerns, etc.), your service quotient in the present moment drops way down. When you focus your attention in optimum directions (the present moment, good feelings in your heart, positive attitudes toward others, etc.), you shift into a more friendly, helpful mood that customers respond to. Here are the four primary directions in which you can choose to focus your attention that will immediately brighten your empathy charge.

1. Focus on the present moment: Most people typically focus their attention on their own inner thoughts, imaginations, worries, dreams, memories, strategies, and so forth – and all of these mental functions take their attention away from the present moment, into the past or the future. Unfortunately for customer satisfaction, when your attention is gone from the present moment, you're not really aware of the customer at all – and therefore not truly available to them.

The first step you always need to make, to ensure that you're "here and now" in the present moment, is to move through a simple but powerful cognitive-shifting process that brings you fully into the present moment where all experience and interaction take place.

2. Focus on your heart: For a great many reasons, most people are not focused on the feelings in their heart. They're focused on the thoughts, images, memories, and imaginings constantly running through their minds. Unless you learn how to shift fast from head to heart focus, customers will experience this lack of warmth from you – and react to it. When your attention is not focused in the region of your heart, at that moment you'll be experienced as a "heartless" person – with serious consequences for customer experience and bonding.

Before an encounter with a client, customer, or any other significant person in your life, it's essential to know a focusing method that instantly takes your attention from head to heart – literally. This is a surefire, guaranteed process for making positive contact with a person.

3. Focus on feeling good: Once again, we find in studies that people fail to focus on their choice of feeling good in their bodies in the present moment. Feeling good is a choice, and if we have mental and emotional habits that focus on bad feelings and upsetting thoughts and memories and imaginations, then we hold ourselves locked in bad feelings rather than good feelings. And, clearly, if we're feeling bad we're not going to help clients and customers feel good.

In preparation for a business or social encounter, it's essential to consciously choose to shift from feeling bad to feeling good.

Of course, in some extreme situations we can't instantly make this shift – but you'll be surprised at how good you can get at choosing to feel good, and then almost instantly shifting into good feelings. All you need is the recognition that you do have the choice to aim your attention in bad- or good-feeling directions, and then perform a particular cognitive-shifting process than enables you to act on this choice.

4. Focus on your positive intent: Most people usually do not hold in mind their positive "intent" for a given situation. Intent is the psychological partner of one's focus of attention – it's your cognitive statement of what you want to accomplish in any given moment of your life. And, if your habitual statement of intent isn't appropriate for the present situation, you won't be able to achieve the opportunity of the present moment. Specifically, if your intent is to manipulate a person rather than to help that person get what they need, your empathy quotient will drop very low, and the customer will react negatively.

The fourth empathy variable requires that you consciously state your positive intent before a sales or service engagement so that you aim your focus of intent directly where it will best serve you.

MENTAL TOOLS

How can you learn to quickly redirect your mind's focus of attention and intent so that you shift your awareness and emotions in directions that optimize business encounters? Cognitive science has developed a new approach to managing your mind, employing powerful "focus phrases" that I'll be teaching you, some of them drawn from my basic mind-management method and some specific to this particular "empathy boost" program. Your easy job is to memorize these primary statements of intent, and then use them before, during, and after every business encounter.

Focus phrases are a natural extension of how your mind works in general. For instance, when you feel hungry in your stomach, this physical experience stimulates your mind to reflect upon what to do to satisfy your hunger. Thoughts and imaginations come to mind, and quite soon you develop a clear and verbal intent so that your mind actually says to itself, "I want to stand up and walk into the kitchen and get myself a sandwich." This is clearly a focus phrase that you say to yourself, usually almost subliminally. Once your mind states its intent, then your body responds to the verbal statement and you go into action to accomplish your intent.

It's the same with anything you do in life. Except for the

most basic physiological functions, there is always a fleeting thought or mental image, a statement of intent that motivates you to go into action directly toward what you want to accomplish. In preparing for an encounter in sales and service, indeed in any business situation, you want to operate basically in the same way.

> My motto in all this work is, "Say it – do it!" State your intent clearly, and then allow those words to focus your attention and stimulate related action to achieve your goal.

What general statement might best express your desired intent as you prepare to meet with a customer or co-worker? Assuming that positive customer experience is the key to a satisfied, loyal customer, how about this:

"I'M GOING TO BE FRIENDLY AND CHEERFUL, LISTEN WITHOUT MANIPULATION, AND HELP SATISFY THIS PERSON'S NEEDS."

This is a good beginning statement of intent, but it's a bit too long and it covers several different themes. I will be teaching you variations upon this general statement, focus phrases that will directly stimulate inner emotional shifting and a rapid uplifting of your mood and empathic focusing of your intent. Specifically, for each of the four empathy variables mentioned above, I will be teaching you a specific focus phrase of great import.

What's important to remember here in the beginning, in learning to activate the true power of focus phrases, is that you don't just think the thought. You "say to yourself" the words – so that the words move from just a mental thought to a physical action or statement of intent.

> You don't have to say the words out loud – it's best to say them "to yourself" so that you feel the words on your lips and tongue and in your throat, but don't vocalize them in sound.

Here's the key psychological point. When you approach someone without clarifying your intent at this level, chances are very high that you will have other thoughts in your mind that determine the quality of the encounter. And, all too often, these thoughts will be stressful, worried, judgmental, and otherwise unhelpful, to say the least. In fact, it's actually dangerous to let your unconscious mind determine where you're focusing your intent in business engagements. Most of the time, you will have negative attitudes grumbling in the back of your mind – and these habitual reactions and expectations will pollute your present-moment emotional presence.

This is why much of this book focuses on teaching you to consciously employ these new cognitive tools before, during, and after a business encounter – so that you take control of your intent and direct your attention specifically where it will serve you (and your client) best.

There is a vast amount of psychological research supporting the logic and power of focus phrases, but you don't need to comprehend the complexity of the dynamic of the method in order to gain full access to its power – any more than you need to fully comprehend how the engine in your car works in order to turn the key and power off down the road. You'll immediately feel the power of the focus phases by memorizing them and using them in work situations, or any interpersonal situation you find yourself in. Say it – do it!

Let's now take a closer look at the four key empathy variables and begin learning their four respective focus phrases that will turn your mind's attention instantly in positive directions.

Present-Moment Focus

In order to relate and listen with empathy to a customer, you obviously need to "be here" in the present moment rather than lost in thoughts about the past or the future. In this regard, psychologically, your mind has several different modes in which it can operate, four different directions that it can aim your focus of attention. Your basic question is always: Which of these four modes of consciousness am I going to focus on right now?

1. You can focus on the past, remembering and reliving the vast assortment of memories that you've accumulated during your life.

2. You can focus on the future, imagining things that might happen to you or conjuring up fantasies and daydreams.

3. You can focus on pure thought and lose yourself in thinking mode, which is abstract and outside the space-time dimension.

4. You can focus on present-moment experience happening right now as a sensory, perceptual event in your body and emotions.

All four of these levels of consciousness are needed in equal balance for a full life. But, when it's time to engage in a business or social interaction of any kind, you will definitely do best if you consciously shift your attention away from the past, the future, and abstract thought, and aim your attention directly toward the present moment and your bodily experience in the here and now – otherwise, you're just not going to be "here" for the other person.

You know the bothersome feeling of relating with someone who's mostly lost in their own thoughts and unrelated memories and imaginations – it's no fun at all. So first and foremost, make sure you don't do that to a customer or colleague. Instead, actively choose just before an encounter (and also throughout that encounter) to consciously bring your awareness fully into the present moment – and keep it there!

I've studied not only the scientific approach to this "present moment" challenge, but also the ancient meditative wisdom and techniques as well. Throughout all world cultures, a prime value has been placed on mental, meditative techniques that help us regain and maintain awareness in the present moment.

> Why is this present moment fixation universal? Because everything that happens in your life happens in the present moment.

For instance, notice that your present moment sensory experience is where you receive absolutely all of your inputs that plug you into the world around you. When you meet someone, if you're not tuned into their physical presence in the here and now, you're going to miss most of their cues as to who they are, how they feel, what they're thinking, and what their needs are. And if you miss these perceptual cues, you're obviously not going to be able to respond and be of service – it's, in essence, that simple.

What is the fast track to waking up to the present moment? Here's 30 years of research in one paragraph. You need to redirect your focus of attention specifically to the most immediate event happening here in the present moment, hold your focus of attention primarily on that experience – and then expand your awareness to include everything else happening around you.

Specifically, you're going to want to stay aware of your own breathing while you tune into all the sensory inputs you're receiving from your client or customer. And to do this, all you need to do is say the following essential focus phrase to yourself:

"I FEEL THE AIR FLOWING IN AND OUT OF MY NOSE."

This first focus phrase will serve as your breath anchor. Whenever you turn your mind's full attention to the sensations being caused by air flowing in and out of your nose, you will shift instantly away from thoughts and memories and imaginations toward the primary sensory event that sustains your life moment to moment in the here and now.

> By saying this first focus phrase to yourself, you "wake up" in the present moment and activate the precise mental function that will enable you to respond with empathy to the person you're meeting.

Feel free to begin experimenting right now with the core process of turning your mind's attention toward the sensation of the air flowing in and out of your nose. Just say to yourself the focus phrase, "I feel the air flowing in and out of my nose," and let the words work their magic. At first what you feel might be subtle, but the more and more effectively you practice, the words will direct your attention where you've stated you want it to go.

Try it again . . . Say it – do it!

"I FEEL THE AIR FLOWING IN AND OUT OF MY NOSE."

Awareness itself is a remarkable quality of the mind – it's our very core of being. When we aren't aware, we simply aren't here. When our awareness is low, we're hardly here. But, our awareness has the amazing quality of being able to expand . . . and expand more . . . and expand still more.

You know that feeling of being vibrantly alive and alert, when you seem to be aware of your whole body at once and tuned into the whole world around you. In this expanded state of awareness, you're in peak condition to participate in the world. You're in the zone, you're spontaneous and friendly and powerful. The more aware you are, the more able you are to share empathy with those around you – and in this expanded state of awareness, naturally your customers will enjoy you and want to return to be with you again.

Notice how your awareness naturally and quite effortlessly expands when you become aware of your breathing. The first focus phrase expands your awareness to include your nose and your head. The second focus phrase that I'm going to teach will expand your awareness to include also the breathing movements in your chest, hands, and down lower in your belly. Suddenly you experience a sense of three-dimensional volume inside your body – and with this experience you pop into the present moment and tune also into the world around you.

Say to yourself, "I feel the air flowing in and out of my nose," and experience that expansion of your awareness for a breath or two. Then say to yourself, "I also feel the movements in my chest and belly as I breathe," and sure enough, your awareness will expand effortlessly so that you're aware of your head, chest, and belly all at once.

This is "consciousness expansion" in a nutshell, and it's your most valuable boost for shifting instantly into the perfect mode for relating with customers. What you're doing at deep levels with this simple two-sentence refocusing process is breaking free from the grip of habitual worries and manipulative thoughts and tuning into where the action's really happening. When you shift from thought to experience, from inner ruminations to perceptual sensory awareness, you make the greatest leap of consciousness possible. You bring yourself back into engagement with the world around you.

Throughout this book I'll return to this primary statement – that always first and foremost, make sure you are focused fully in the present moment, both before and during a business encounter of any kind. This is the crucial first step, and when you only have time to make this first step, it will suffice. Be here for your customer and your customer will be grateful!

Heart Focus

Once you begin your awareness expanding into more complete engagement with the present moment, the next natural expansion, beyond your breathing experience, is to include whatever feelings you find in your heart. You'll notice that you can't really separate feelings in your heart from the way you're breathing – your emotions are, after all, expressed directly through your breathing. So, it's best to include your breathing experience as part of your heart experience.

There's no question – empathy is a quality of experience found in the heart, not the head. We saw that empathy is not just a lofty thought or ideal. It's an emotional experience, and felt most clearly and often as a positive emotion in the heart region. Empathic relating is a heart-to-heart interaction that is experienced through your power of expanded awareness in the present moment.

> If you want to tune into empathic feelings, the primary act you can make is to shift your focus of attention from your head to your heart.

This might seem rather simplistic, but it's just the opposite. All you need to learn how to do, and get really good at, is turning your mind's attention to the area in your chest and becoming more and more receptive to the feelings you find happening in that region of your body.

But here's the catch – most people have a difficult time performing this seemingly simple cognitive-shifting action. If at first you find this expansion of awareness to include the feelings in your heart difficult or seemingly even impossible to accomplish, you're in with the large majority of people. Most people, and yes, more men than women, do have great difficulty making contact with the feelings in their hearts. It's sad but true – and it's time to do something about it. Not only does a lack of heart awareness influence your personal and family life, it without question limits your business success as well – especially if you're regularly engaged in sales, service, or teamwork situations.

This was George's primary dilemma. As a macho man, he'd inherited his father's "manly" stance of blocking his softer, more compassionate feelings almost entirely. He was tough and dominant and not vulnerable to the feelings of the heart, which he considered a sign of weakness. The truth was he was scared to death of his more emotional inner feelings. And, the consequences of this were seen throughout his daily life. His wife was unhappy because she didn't feel loved, his children felt he didn't care about them, and most of his colleagues thought of him as a cold, ruthless guy that they could not feel close to or trust. He was able to manipulate people like a pro, but he couldn't share the basic ingredients of true fellowship and community – warm, compassionate emotions, trustful behavior, and a willingness to truly be of service rather than always grabbing for himself.

I've worked with hundreds of clients very similar to George, who weren't seriously neurotic or in need of long-term therapy. All they needed was a new vision of their own lives, and the mental tools to implement that vision.

And what is the vision? Living a life where you're regularly in touch with and responsive to the feelings you find in your heart.

Of course, with people like George, there's always a reservoir of blocked emotions that comes from a lifetime of sealing yourself off from bad feelings. If you find that you have a hard time turning your attention to the feelings in your heart, to the center of empathy in your body, chances are high that you're also afraid to open up and discover what feelings actually do live there.

But, look realistically for a moment at the alternative – living the rest of your life shut off from your own feelings. This is real hell on earth, and a great many people are living in this emotional hellhole. I recommend taking all measures to get yourself out of this hole if you're stuck in it. And here's the basic process that will get the job done, if you'll devote just two minutes to the process a number of times a day.

1. Relax a moment, get comfortable – and then say to yourself, "I feel the air flowing in and out of my nose." Be silent and allow those words to remain in your mind as they direct your attention to the present-moment experience happening with your breathing. Each time you say these words and let them redirect your focus of attention, you'll get better at the process . . . until you master the shift.

2. While still remaining aware of the sensations of your breathing in your nose and throat, expand your awareness by saying to yourself, "I'm also aware of the movements in my chest and belly as I breathe." Allow the impact of these words to generate that expansion of your awareness to include your head, chest, and belly all at once. It's this "all at once" expanded awareness that brings you fully into the present moment.

    When you focus on two or more sensations happening at the same time, your thinking mind instantly shuts down and becomes quiet. This is how this simple process generates a great shift in consciousness.

You cannot focus on past-future thoughts and sensory events in the present moment, at the same time. So, you are consciously choosing to let go of the past and the future — and to wake up in the present moment.

3. Now you're ready to expand another notch and, without hesitation or anticipation, simply say to the third focus phrase to yourself:

"I'M ALSO AWARE OF THE FEELINGS IN MY HEART."

Say it – do it! In a rather matter-of-fact way, just go ahead and be aware of whatever feelings you encounter in your heart region.

Every time you do this, it will be new – you never have the same experience twice. Time marches on, and each moment is unique and new. What you find in your heart is always new as well. That's the genuine magic of present-moment awareness. It's always new.

So, please don't start anticipating what you'll experience or try to "make yourself feel" anything at all. Just observe and experience how the power of your mind's attention begins to wake up your potential to feel in your heart, even if initially what you feel might be a mess of negative emotions or even numbness. What's important is making the first step – getting your attention in the habit of turning toward your heart.

Do this over and over, and don't be concerned about what you find. Each time you look to your heart, you'll discover a slight change, a beginning of new feelings – and, step by step, more warmth and expansion, more space, and more relaxation. Don't dwell on heart fixation – just exercise your ability to turn your attention there more and more often.

> There's no question that you need to become more heart centered if you want to express more empathy at work. And that means you must focus regularly on the region and feelings of your heart.

Much of this book is devoted to advancing your ability to tap into good feelings in your heart. We're going to explore solid ways to encourage good feelings, heal bad ones, and carry a positive charge of friendly feelings with you wherever you go. For now, we're at the beginning of this journey – start with the primary act of regularly turning your attention to your heart. The rest will follow.

> Even while you're reading these words (and for the rest of this book), see what begins to happen if you also stay aware of the air flowing in and out of your nose . . . and the movements in your chest and belly as you breathe . . . and also the feelings in your heart – right now!

Just like you must go jogging or to the gym or do any other kind of exercise to stay in shape and advance yourself, exercising with these new focus phrases is a discipline. If you read this book and then never move yourself through the focus-phrase process, quite naturally you will gain nothing. So, regularly exercise your mind's attention muscle. Shift often and more and more quickly to present-moment awareness! That's the direct path to customer satisfaction.

Focus on Good Feelings

When you're feeling bad, which means that you are focused on negative thoughts and emotions, you're not going to be any fun to be around. But, when you're feeling good, which means focusing on positive thoughts and emotions, you're a pleasure to be with. Mood management is all about realizing that you have this core choice of feeling bad or feeling good.

> Once you see that you have the choice, of course, there's really no choice. Who wants to feel bad when they can feel good? And yet a great many of us, not realizing we have the choice to shift from bad to good feelings at will, go around sabotaging our work lives by staying in "downer" moods.

Please notice that your experience of feeling bad or good is a direct function of your sensory physical body. Feelings are experienced not in your mind, nor are they experienced in the past or the future. By definition, feelings are found only in the here and now of your senses, plain and simple. That's why you must choose to focus in the present moment at sensory levels, to actually experience feeling good.

Note this as well. Contrary to the average person's assumption, most of your emotions are stimulated not by what's happening around you in your physical perceptual environment. You might actually blame the external world for your mood shifts, but psychological studies show quite clearly that your emotions are stimulated mostly by the thoughts you're habitually thinking, the memories running through your mind, and your worries or dreams of the future.

> Emotions are hormonal and physiological responses to either what happens around you or to the thoughts and images you fixate on in your mind. An external event might push a particular emotional button, but it's your recurrent thought fixations that block you into a negative mood.

Traditional therapy is all about trying to help one come to terms with negative things that happened in the past, so that through deep insight and understanding of the past, one can feel better in the present. This psychotherapeutic approach demonstrates only quite limited success. My approach to therapy has evolved over the years in other, more effective directions. To my knowledge, nobody ever actually eliminates trauma from the past. When they recover, they simply stop fixating upon the past and learn to focus more fully on the present moment.

During recent years of my therapy career, I have worked more as a teacher than a therapist because I spend most of the time teaching my clients what I'm teaching you here – pragmatic tools you can use to shift out of bad moods (anger, depression, anxiety, confusion, boredom, hopelessness, etc.) at will and into more productive and fulfilling moods.

> The trick lies in realizing you have the choice of focusing on negative or positive themes, and then employing particular focus phrases that state your intent of where you want to refocus your almighty power of attention.

And, whenever you realize you don't feel good and want to shift into more enjoyable feelings, the first step is to focus your attention away from all thoughts and toward your physical presence in the here and now. Don't spend another moment disconnected from your sense resource of pleasure. Go to where the pleasure is found.

The three focus phrases I've just taught you may seem quite simple when you are first exposed to them, but you will soon discover on your own why they are the most effective means developed to date for generating this shift from thought to experience. They get the job done, and certainly in the business world, the shortest, quickest, most effective solution is the solution we want.

The following fourth focus phrase springs forth from the first three and states clearly your intent to focus on the good feelings you find in your body, rather than on your negative emotions. Here it is:

"I LET GO OF BAD FEELINGS AND CHOOSE TO FEEL GOOD."

At any given moment you have many physical places in or on your body that don't necessarily feel good. Plus, you have emotional situations that, when focused on, will make you feel bad. You have worries of the future that can totally ruin your day if you let them take over your mind. And, you have a host of upsetting experiences from the past that are more than willing to dominate your experience in a most negative way.

But, at the very same time, you have loads of places in and on your body that feel good and that have the potential to feel good instantaneously. You have positive emotional situations that warm your heart if you think about them, and you have dreams of the future and fond memories of the past that can further improve your mood if you focus on them instead of the bad things.

There's an ego voice inside you that's constantly talking. Out of habit, this voice is often fixated on thoughts about your worries and bad experiences, which, in turn, provoke negative feelings in your body. To counteract this chronic negative chatter, you're learning to make certain statements of intent that fill your mind with a new consciously chosen focus – in this case, toward feeling good rather than feeling bad. And you make it by saying often to yourself, "I let go of bad feelings and choose to feel good."

Say it – do it!

Positive Intent

There's a final step needed to complete your preparations before a meeting or encounter at work – the step of clarifying in your own heart and mind what you intend to accomplish with the meeting. Let's return to our example scenario, George. George wasn't a bad guy. He wasn't an out-and-out crook trying to steal what he could grab from clients. His own self-image was quite positive, which is why he was so flabbergasted by the negative feedback his former clients gave in the customer satisfaction surveys.

> George's problem was that he was carrying a mostly unconscious intent into his sales encounters, which was poisoning his relationships with his clients.

Rather than relating to the world through trust and sharing and service, the attitude that had been pounded into George's mind by both his father and culture in general was that it's a ruthless world out there, unfair and dangerous – and you must constantly keep your guard up, be stronger than the other guy, and push your way to success . . . without ever letting your feelings get in your way.

> In other words, George was operating out of fear and distrust, rather than focusing on empathy and trust.

If you look at George's situation carefully from a psychological point of view, you'll see that there's a definite choice involved in how we perceive the world around us – and both views of the world can be substantiated by data and experience. It's all a matter of what you want to focus on – the negative view or the positive view.

Once you evaluate the choice closely, you'll realize that in most situations, the negative choice is pointless. Who wants to go around feeling chronically threatened, defensive, distrustful, and all the rest of the basic fear-based mentality when you can choose to feel safe and expansive and trustful of life? If, indeed, what you focus on is what tends to manifest in your life, then it's actually self-destructive to focus on the negative. And, pleasure obviously lies with the second choice, not the first. We're built to gravitate toward pleasure and avoid pain – so why don't we?

> The culprit is usually fear-based childhood conditioning and certain cultural programming that poison our hearts and minds against living our lives focused on trust and love and enjoyment.

George discovered that when he let go of his negative one-liners about having to overpower his clients to get a sale and focused on positive one-liners that shifted him into being truly of service to his clients, everything went better for him. When he said to himself just before a meeting, "My intent is to be friendly and cheerful, to listen without manipulation, and to help satisfy this person's needs," he relaxed and enjoyed the meeting. By being fully attuned to his clients' needs he was able to help satisfy them – and make some friends in the bargain. That's the wise path in all your encounters at work.

> As we'll explore in depth later, when you meet with someone, you do best to focus on that person's positive dimensions so that you bring those dimensions to the forefront of the meeting, rather than anticipating all the negative possibilities and provoking that dimension.

For now, even as you read these words, remember that staying aware of the air flowing in and out of your nose or mouth keeps you in the present moment – where life is actually happening. Expanding to also be aware of the movements in your chest and belly drops you down into a greater awareness of your entire body here in the present moment. And, expanding again to include the feelings in your heart helps you meet people heart to heart and establish good feelings between the two of you.

And now we are ready to activate that overall statement of intent with which we began this chapter:

"I AM READY TO BE FRIENDLY AND CHEERFUL, TO LISTEN WITHOUT MANIPULATION, AND TO HELP SATISFY THIS PERSON'S NEEDS."

As mentioned before, the seemingly simple process that you are learning in this book is based on years of rather complex psychological development. For instance, if you state your primary business intent (of being ready to be friendly and cheerful, to listen without manipulation, and to help satisfy your customer's needs) before you have moved through the first three focus phrases that wake you up to good, heartfelt emotions in your heart and body, your statement of intent will pack very little power.

You must tune into your breathing experience, focus on your heart, and give yourself permission to feel good before you express your intent to interact successfully with another person. I should point out that after a few weeks of practice, as soon as you focus toward your breathing experience, you will very quickly and deeply move through the entire process. But always, one way or another – you will need to be aware of your breathing and your heart before stating your business intent.

In the very first days of training in this Listening with Empathy method, you will almost surely have an experience similar to George's. Through a bit of repetition and discipline, and the natural tendency of the heart to be responsive emotionally, George began waking up to slight and then more demonstrative feelings in his heart – sometimes just a sudden softness and warmth when he was with his boys at a football game, or tenderness when with his wife, and finally at work as well – feeling relaxed companionship and empathy for his co-workers. And then, just as he hoped, he began making genuine heart contact with clients.

You have a beginning sense of action you can take to prepare yourself for a successful and enjoyable business meeting. In the next chapter, we'll explore an additional step that I also taught George, which further helped his progress.

Summary of "Sensory Wake-Up" Process

For quick review, here is what you've learned thus far. When you have just a minute or less to prepare for an encounter, memorize and say the focus phrases to yourself on each new exhale, and experience the impact of the words on your inner experience on each inhale.

First of all, you must remember that you do know this method for rapidly shifting your attention into the present moment and for waking up your heartfelt empathic feelings. Then, you must remember the words of the first two focus phrases, and let those words lead your attention to your breath experience.

1. "I feel the air flowing in and out of my nose."

2. "I also feel the movements in my chest and belly."

Then, remember the words of the feeling good, heart focus phrases that guide your attention to your center of empathy and pleasure.

3. "I'm also aware of the feelings in my heart."

4. "I let go of bad feelings and choose to feel good."

Finally, you can state the core intent that fully activates your sales and service mood and power.

5. "I am ready to be friendly and cheerful, to listen without manipulation, and to help satisfy this person's needs."

CHAPTER 2

BOOST YOUR EMPATHY CHARGE

Karen, in many ways, was the opposite of George. Rather than being one of many mid-range employees she was a senior executive in a large corporation, with responsibilities that had an impact on the future of her entire company. But, in a way, she was still in sales because every day she had to meet people and pitch ideas and programs to various committees – trying to sell her ideas both through the merit of the ideas and through the power and charisma of her personal presence.

But, in contrast to George, Karen's difficulty with her emotions wasn't that she was numb in her heart and shut down emotionally – her problem was that she was too emotional, overly moody, and often charged with inappropriate feelings for the situation at hand.

Her mind was constantly muttering about one worry or another, and she tended to carry grudges and apprehensions.

Caught up in thoughts and imaginings that provoked the opposite of empathy, Karen often walked into a meeting with a chip on her shoulder or a nagging worry about something unrelated to the meeting. At other times she'd be at low emotional ebb, empty of confidence, and close to tears.

Karen came to me not because a higher-up had criticized her performance at work or because customers had made negative comments on how she related with them. She came for training because she realized her moodiness was limiting her success at work and sabotaging her personal relationships. At first she was a bit defensive about the whole idea of mood management – she was a passionate woman who didn't want to become rigid and cold like so many of her colleagues. I explained to her that mood management as I approach it would do the opposite of inhibiting her passions – it would set her free to fully express emotions that were appropriate for the situation. By gaining control of her emotions, she'd be able to express them more fully when the setting was proper.

Based on this assurance, Karen began avidly memorizing, and then putting to regular hourly use the beginning process I've just taught you. At first she complained that the method was too simplistic for her, that she had better things to do with her time than sit around and watch her breathing. She quickly realized that, indeed, changes in her awareness and her emotions did happen when she used a bit of discipline with the training. And so she learned to turn her attention to her breathing experience in her nose and chest and belly, and the feelings in her heart.

> In a week or so, Karen found that she could easily make the shift – from being lost in thoughts that chronically stimulated her emotions to finding peace of mind and good feelings in her body in the here and now.

As you'll also find, in some instances this basic method works adequately well – you pause for just a minute or so, take charge of your mind's focus of attention, and shift to positive action. This is always the first step toward making sure your emotions are appropriate to the situation you're in – tune into the present moment of that situation, put aside past and future events, and give the present moment a chance to impact your heart and your behavior.

But, Karen's moody thoughts were quite deeply ingrained. Like most of us, she carried an entire collection of negative judgmental attitudes, beliefs, and one-liners that would quickly reinstate themselves, pulling her attention away from the present moment and back to her pet peeves. What to do? Time for the second round of the Listening with Empathy program!

PSYCHOLOGICAL JUDO

What I've taught you thus far has dealt primarily with your perceptual experience – how to shift more fully into sensory awareness of your physical presence in the here and now. Specifically, you've learned how to quickly tune into sensations in your nose, throat, chest, belly, and heart. Often, that's all the time you have before an encounter, and it can in itself work wonders when applied to any situation in life.

There's another dimension to mood management that can also greatly augment your success. I've described various aspects of this "attitude shifting" process in many of my books and online courses, and now I would like to apply the basic method to our particular "empathy boost" challenge.

There are four negative psychological habits that most of us were programmed with during childhood that directly inhibit our ability to shift into empathic feelings and warm heart contact: 1) fixating on worrisome memories and imaginations; 2) thinking judgmental thoughts; 3) indulging in self-condemnation; and 4) keeping the heart chronically closed to emotional engagement.

For years I employed complex therapy methods for helping clients overcome these habits, until I realized there's a better way to approach the situation – using psychological judo rather than karate. Rather than using opposing force to actively push negative thoughts out of our minds, we can redirect existing energies and habits to accomplish our goals. Instead of trying to make our minds stop saying negative things, we're going to give our minds positive things to say.

For each of our moods and emotions, there are two opposite attitude poles on which we can focus. We can be bored or excited, worried or confident, judgmental or accepting, disturbed or peaceful, stressed or healthy, depressed or happy, angry or friendly, and coldhearted or empathic. For each of these mental/emotional conditions there are particular thoughts and attitudes and beliefs that stimulate the negative, and equal and opposite thoughts and beliefs that stimulate the positive. We tend to swing back and forth from one emotional condition to another – negative to positive and back to negative – depending on the thoughts that we habitually allow to fill our minds.

This is the short explanation of why we are plagued by moods – we're actually provoking them ourselves by the thoughts and related images and memories that flow mostly subliminally through our minds.

The basic thrust of cognitive therapy, as you perhaps know, teaches clients to replace habitual negative one-liners with more positive one-liners. This is the only scientifically proven therapy technique that consistently works – and it works because it gets to the core cause of the problem. The technique is nothing new. Four thousand years ago, ancient yogic masters wrote dissertations on this very same reality of the human mind. As Buddha clearly pointed out, human beings run torture chambers in their own minds.

To directly counteract the four primary psychological habits that interfere with our empathy expression, my colleagues and I have developed equal and opposite one-liners that you can begin using immediately to confidently take control of your moods when they are inappropriate to a work situation.

Quite different from positive affirmations, these focus phrases don't state some dreamy, unrealistic wish that you want to have magically happen. Rather, they simply aim your full attention in realistic emotional directions that you already have in your repertoire – and by focusing in that positive direction, they help you shift step by step toward positive moods and experiences.

The dynamic is fully proven by cognitive science; that is, when you actively state the emotional or attitudinal direction you want to move in, your inner system will predictably respond to your suggestion and focus in the emotional direction you choose. Let's take an example that you've already begun to learn – choosing to focus on feeling good rather than feeling bad.

Who wouldn't like to feel great all of the time? That's the ideal, and you do in general already know how to feel good. In fact, we've already introduced the focus phrase that is always available to you. You are always free to say to yourself, "I let go of bad feelings and choose to feel good." You say the words to yourself on a quiet exhale, and then on your next inhale allow those words to reverberate throughout your system and generate a positive emotional effect inside you.

Being a sophisticated, intellectual woman, Karen at first scoffed at the seeming simplicity of stating her intent in just one line, and then experiencing immediate results. With you as with her, all I ask is that you experiment with this focus-phrase technology for just a week or two to discover from the inside out the power of this method. You're learning how to tap your existing natural ability to feel good by using a clear, positive statement of intent.

> You're employing emotional pressure and energy inside you to move you in a desired direction. That's the judo part of the process – taking advantage of your natural yearning to feel good at work, to provoke a positive emotional shift in that direction.

You can also say a shorter version of the focus phase:

"I GIVE MYSELF PERMISSION TO FEEL GOOD."

The magic of all this is that, indeed, by saying the words to yourself, something does happen! When you give yourself permission to feel good, you don't necessarily instantly feel totally great – but each time you'll experience a slight shift in that direction. Each time you'll get better at the shift and go further. And, that slight shift experienced ten or more times a day will begin adding up to a major new brightness in your mood and warmth in your heart.

I'm not offering you unrealistic hope. This Listening with Empathy process is definitely incremental, but with a bit of practice it does deliver results. Realistically, we don't just suddenly and totally transcend all of our negative attitudes and moods and become enlightened. Rather, we grow and heal and improve step by step.

This is why I've designed this method around short modules of experience that you repeat many times a day. If you do your part and dedicate just a minute or two every hour to making the process a new habit in your life, in weeks you will truly transform your moods and noticeably improve your empathic presence at work. Either through memorizing the process as it's written in this book or using the effortless audio guidance provided online, you can gain the tools and apply them to your life.

THE FOUR PILLARS OF EMPATHY

Let's learn the four primary "attitude adjustment" focus phrases that point your mind's full attention in the empathic directions you choose to encourage in your life. Each time you say these sentences to yourself, you'll actively move your mood in your chosen direction. Remember always to first move through the initial awareness wake-up process taught in chapter 1, so that you're "here" in the present moment, where real growth is possible. Remain aware of your breathing, your heart, and your whole-body good feelings. Then, advance through the four following attitude-shifting steps that will fully prepare you for a business encounter of any kind.

Pillar 1: Let Your Worries Go

There's nothing more destructive to an encounter with a client or customer than broadcasting anxiety or worry in the meeting. Everyone is susceptible to catching this negative emotion, and if you're locked into thoughts and expectations that are fear based, you're going to contaminate the customer with these negative feelings.

Worrying is a function of your mind: thoughts, images, and imaginings that stimulate physical reactions you then experience as anxiety – tense breath, weak muscles, confused mind, unfocused attention, apprehensive expectations, suspicious thoughts, and so forth. Before you meet with someone, be it an insurance client in George's situation or maybe even the head of the board in Karen's situation, be sure that you take charge of your mind and state your intent clearly related to worried feelings. Say it – do it!

"MY MIND IS QUIET, MY EMOTIONS CALM."

The first few times you say these words and state this intent, nothing much will happen. You haven't yet exercised and strengthened your power to do what you're saying. But I assure you, after a few times of saying these words and stating this clear intent, you'll find that something does happen inside you. You will begin to let go of worried thoughts and shift into a more peaceful feeling in your mind. Your breathing will relax as you enter more fully into enjoyment of the present moment.

You've done what you can to take charge of your mind, state your intent to be free of worries, and quell your anxious thoughts. Every time you stay to this intent, you'll get better at it and shift further in the direction you aim your intent toward.

Pillar 2: Stop Being Judgmental

If fear is the number one enemy of empathic feelings (you can't be in a state of fear and feel love at the same time), then judgment is the second primary villain to deal with if you want to shift into friendly mode with someone. After all, who wants to spend time with someone who's judging them negatively? What customer wants to relate with an employee who is harboring thoughts such as "Gee, what a fat guy!" or "This person looks really dumb" or "I hate people who dress like that" or some other prejudice?

Being judged is a psychic attack – and customers feel this attack even if it isn't stated. New research (see my website for documentation) has actually shown that our minds and hearts do broadcast energetic information that the minds and hearts of others pick up and subliminally respond to. The inner thoughts you think about a client have been shown scientifically to radiate outward and impact that person.

So, before you enter into an engagement with someone, it's vital to consciously clear the air and state the positive intent of letting go of your habitual judgments. To do this, in preparation for the encounter, you say to yourself the following focus phrase:

"I HONOR AND RESPECT THE PERSON I'M MEETING WITH."

As mentioned earlier, I'm not expecting you to totally shift and entirely accept another person the first time you try this method. All I'm asking is that you begin moving yourself in the direction of full acceptance. You have to start where you are and advance step by step. You'll find that right away, if you've first gone through the process to quiet your mind through "present-moment" shifting, that most of your judgmental thoughts are already quiet – this method, like I said, builds incrementally from the first focus phrase you say to the next.

Most judgment is based on fear – that's the nature of judgment psychologically; it's there to protect you from a possible danger. If you've already stated that you let go of your worries, then it becomes a lot easier to accept the person you're meeting without judgment. You let go of distrust because you're not afraid of this person. And, with the fear gone, you can simply take this person in without judging.

> Hold in mind that when you're judging someone it's difficult to experience this person just as they are – that's what prejudice is all about.

So, begin to exercise your power to give the other person the benefit of the doubt. Experience who they really are rather than draping stereotypical judgments on them.

Pillar 3: Stop the Self-Sabotage

Now we come to perhaps the greatest, most damaging judgment function of the mind – that of self-judgment. If you are thinking (even at subliminal levels) just before an encounter that you're no good, that you're not likable, that you're a failure, that the meeting is going to turn out badly, then you're going to bring these negative vibes with you into the meeting and pollute the entire situation.

I grew up with this problem of expecting people not to like

me, or to ignore me, or to even be hostile toward me – so I know how this feels. I also know the only sure path that leads quickly from negative to positive. Over and over, simply state the positive desire and intent that you feel in your heart.

Of course you want to feel love in your heart for your own self. Who doesn't? There's nothing that feels better than self-love! So, rather than looking to the outside world to provide you with the love you need to flourish, begin giving it to yourself. After all, no one can truly receive love from another person if they don't love themselves first. Unlovable people are people who deny themselves love.

So, go into action regardless of where you are on this self-love/self-hate scale. State the direction you want to move in, and each time you make this statement you'll move in that direction. This is the sum total of successful therapy, and you can do it without the therapist. Here are the words that work best, and of course you can vary them a bit if you find another way to say the same thing:

"I FEEL GOOD TOWARD MY OWN SELF."

Say it – do it! Especially just before a business meeting, don't go into that meeting hitting yourself over the head with an emotional hammer. Go in feeling good in your heart toward your own self. This and only this will enable the people you're meeting with to respond with reciprocal warmth, trust, and acceptance.

Pillar 4: Be Open to Receive

The final mental habit that interferes directly with positive customer experience is the prevailing attitude most people take to work with them, of protecting themselves at emotional levels by keeping their hearts closed and impervious to the emotions of others. You probably know what it's like to meet with someone who doesn't respond at all to your personal warmth or offer of friendship. A great many people are cold fish; they're stone when it comes to receiving the emotional exchange that builds lasting relationships.

I've worked with hundreds of executives who suffer from this habitually non-receptive condition of the heart. Traditionally, the stereotype role model for a business leader was exactly this tough, masculine, invulnerable personality that was "above" human emotions.

Based on the entirely erroneous belief that our emotions lead us astray in decision-making rather than contribute a touch of wisdom to the decision, companies have often hired emotionally constricted leaders who worship the intellect and reject the guidance of their own hearts.

But, in real life, who wants to follow a leader who is heartless? Who wants to do business with someone who feels no compassion or mercy? Who wants to buy a product from a person who is hiding their true heart feelings as they make the deal? This fourth focus phrase encourages your intent to be open and receptive at work.

"I OPEN MY HEART TO RECEIVE FRIENDSHIP AND ENJOY GOOD FEELINGS WITH THIS PERSON."

I know that certain people will initially react with scorn to any talk about "opening my heart" at work. This is talk usually reserved for church groups and touchy-feely New Age encounters, not work situations. But look at the opposite – what if your one-liner before meeting with someone is "I'm going to keep my heart closed and shut down and be unresponsive to this person." That's the standard traditional business stance. If you have inherited this one-liner, then it's going to damage all of your business relationships. So I say, let's talk about the process of maintaining an open heart at work. Let the discussion begin.

Who wants to actively make sure their company stance is an openhearted, receptive one with customers, and who wants to maintain the company's tradition of making sure employees remain coldhearted and unresponsive?

I'm sure the positive one-liner will soon become company policy at your organization, if your company wants to survive and thrive in the new era.

ALL TOGETHER NOW

You now have an overview of the basic "preparation" program that enables you to quickly shift into the optimum mental and emotional condition for a sales or service encounter at work. You can begin practicing and mastering the process and right away begin applying the method at work. Take advantage of the online training program if you learn best through audio instruction.

Even when you have just half a minute, with a bit of training you can quickly move through the process. In fact, I've found that the old adage "more is better" does not necessarily apply to such programs as this. Focus phrases actually have the best impact when you say one of them to yourself, and then pause just for one or two breaths to experience whatever impact the words have on you. Then, rather than dwelling longer on that focus phrase, say the next one to yourself, pause for one to two breaths, and then move on to the next, until you finish the full sequence.

Why does this short-frame timing work best? Because each focus phrase builds on the impact the one before has had on your mind and emotions. And, if you pause too long between sentences, your mind begins drifting – and this is exactly what we don't want to have happen.

So, consider yourself lucky – I'm not asking you to find a free half-hour at work in order to successfully apply this method. In fact, I'm encouraging you to do it fairly quickly and all at once. Following is a succinct summary of the preparation process for quick reference.

THE PREPARATION PROCESS

A: Two-Minute Preparation

1. Say to yourself, "I feel the air flowing in and out of my nose . . ."

   . . . and, as you inhale, tune in fully to this sensory experience.

2. Say to yourself, "I also feel the movements in my chest and belly . . ."

   . . . and expand your awareness to include your whole body.

3. Say to yourself, "I'm aware of the feelings in my heart . . ."

   . . . and breathe into the feelings you find in your heart.

4. Say to yourself, "I give myself permission to feel good . . ."

   . . . and tune into any good feelings you find inside.

5. Say to yourself, "My mind is quiet, my emotions calm . . ."

. . . and enjoy the feeling of inner calm in your mind.

6. Say to yourself, "I honor and respect the person I'm meeting with . . ."

   . . . and let acceptance fill your mind and open your heart.

7. Say to yourself, "I feel good toward my own self . . ."

   . . . and experience the heart feelings these words awaken.

8. Say to yourself, "I'm ready to be friendly and cheerful, to listen without manipulation, and to help satisfy this person's needs . . ."

   . . . and allow these words to resonate throughout your being.

Here are the same eight focus phrases for the two-minute preparation process, grouped for quick reference and memorization.

1. "I feel the air flowing in and out of my nose . . ."

2. "I also feel the movements in my chest and belly . . ."

3. "I'm also aware of the feelings in my heart . . ."

4. "I give myself permission to feel good . . ."

5. "My mind is quiet, my emotions calm . . ."

6. "I honor and respect the person I'm meeting with . . ."

7. "I feel good toward my own self . . ."

8. "I'm ready to be friendly and cheerful

    . . . to listen without manipulation

    . . . and to help satisfy this person's needs . . ."

B: Short, Short

For when you have just a few moments, here's a special version of the process to memorize and use.

1. Say to yourself, "I'm tuned into my breathing . . ."

    . . . and turn your mind's attention to the air flowing in and out of your nose, and the movements in your chest and belly as you breathe.

2. Say to yourself, "I'm also aware of the feelings in my heart . . ."

. . . and let your awareness expand and include whatever's happening in your heart . . . and welcome good feelings in your heart!

3. Say to yourself, "I let go of worries and feel peaceful inside . . ."

   . . . and as the words impact your inner experience, breathe into an expansion of both confidence and pure pleasure.

4. Say "I'm ready to accept, to serve, and to succeed . . ."

   . . . and let each of these key elicitor words . . . accept . . . serve . . . succeed . . . ground you in your primary intent in the coming meeting.

❧

1. "I'm tuned into my breathing . . ."

2. "I'm also aware of the feelings in my heart . . ."

3. "I let go of worries and feel peaceful inside . . ."

4. "I'm ready to accept, to serve, and to succeed . . ."

CHAPTER 3

CREATE ROOM FOR FRIENDSHIP

We're now going to venture into territory almost always over-looked or seriously misunderstood in traditional customer relations training programs. By the end of this chapter you'll realize just how crucial this dimension is for helping you succeed at high levels in customer bonding and also during negotiations, team brainstorming, and all other relationship situations.

Coaches and trainers alike tend to avoid this particular dimension of at-work friendship building because, without a clear understanding of consciousness itself, you can't develop a pragmatic program to augment the "creating room" process.

Behavioral psychology by definition doesn't deal with consciousness; therefore, that standard approach lacks the conceptual framework within which to explain the phenomenon.

What is the phenomenon? It's your ability to expand your consciousness so that you maintain a sense of "open space and free time" as a vital ingredient in your business encounters.

Most people do just the opposite – they rush into a meeting with the feeling that there's no free time or relaxed breathing space available for the meeting beyond the bare minimum needed to get the job done. As you well know, the definition of a pressurized workday means there is no time to waste. This attitude translates into no time to relax for a few moments and allow a customer to relate person to person with the sales or service representative.

It's admittedly difficult to nail down the experience of "free time" in formal experiments, but we all know the feeling of pausing and shifting into a relaxed state where there's room to breathe – room to stop "doing" and enjoy just "being" for a moment.

What's most important for learning how to listen with empathy is that only within this "free breathing space" can two people actually relate at heart levels and discover feelings of companionship and genuine connection.

This is why preparation is so important to success. This

sense of expansive, receptive openness and free time is something that we must first nurture within our own inner experience before it can be shared with a customer. If you fail to maintain a sense of open, available time, your customers aren't going to experience this quality in the meeting – and they'll probably feel slighted.

A nonverbal message is being subtly communicated when you create no free time beyond formal business – the message that you have no real concern for the customer as a human being. You just want to get the deal done – and then be done with the customer. Obviously, this is not good business practice. When it is looked at logically, choosing to create a bit of free time to relate heart to heart with the customer is almost always very good business. But, in traditional sales training, at a non-manipulative level this relaxed receptive quality of consciousness is not taught at all. So, here and now, what can be done?

ROGER'S DILEMMA

Roger was co-owner and manager of an upscale restaurant in Los Angeles that boasted a famous chef and a great location. Important people often came to his restaurant, and he would make the effort to go out and be gracious to them, chatting briefly with small talk to make them feel comfortable and respected. But, there was often an emptiness left in the wake of his short excursions from table to table – because in his mind he really had no time for this chatting.

I'd known Roger from earlier times and had frequented the restaurant myself, and clearly observed the situation. One Monday afternoon when he was off duty, I pointed out to him that after he left a table, I'd noticed that people often would makes faces of displeasure rather than satisfaction. He explained that he was under such time pressure that, of course, it was difficult to be relaxed and genuinely friendly with his customers.

I knew business was sagging at his restaurant, so I pushed deeper. "You pressure your waiters, too," I pointed out. "There's a general feeling of being rushed, and this doesn't make your customers enjoy their meals."

"Hey, you know how the restaurant business is," he retorted.

"I know how many restaurants fail," I said evenly. "And in many cases it's because the employees can't relax and enjoy their work so customers can relax and enjoy the dining experience. When customers aren't given space and time to relax and enjoy the moment, next time they go someplace else."

"But I can't just slow everything down and relax the pace. I'd lose money head over heels if I reduced the pressure on the waiters."

"Roger, you were half-full the last time I was in. That's losing money. What if you granted each waiter just one minute of free time per table to take a deep breath, relax, and enjoy the company of the people they're serving so they can make genuine heart contact with customers?"

"I've trained them to put on a friendly face when they take orders; that's part of the job."

"Yes, but that usually comes across as less than genuine. What about giving your employees the freedom to keep enough breathing space in their own hearts and minds so that they actually feel like they're getting paid to enjoy the present moment – then that will spread to the customers, and everyone benefits."

OPEN SPACE TO BREATHE

That afternoon I taught Roger a short version of what I'm teaching you – the basic process of pausing for just four breaths perhaps once every ten to 20 minutes to regain that positive sense of having free time to relax, recover, and recharge. I showed him that, just before making his rounds of tables, he could pause and consciously shift out of rush gear and give himself permission to enjoy the moment – thus making sure he had free time to make genuine contact with his customers.

There's a basic psychological dynamic in operation here. When Roger was in a hurry (which initially was all the time), his focus of attention was mostly gone from the present moment, off in the future with plans and worries and so forth. In his mind, he was projecting a few seconds or even a few minutes ahead of his body.

In this hurried state of mind, Roger simply could not make heart contact with his customers – because he wasn't there for them at all. He might be physically chatting with them, but emotionally he was gone; therefore, that empty feeling of phony friendship was all that remained.

Roger is a smart man. He quickly understood the logic I was laying out for him. He'd always wondered why his "table trips" left him feeling unsatisfied even though he said all the right things and could act the role with finesse. He was willing to experiment, learn my basic method, and apply it at work. He especially grabbed onto the "open space and free time" one-liner that works so well for high-pressure situations.

Pause, turn your attention to your breathing to regain the present moment – and also focus on your heart. Tune into the sensory experiences coming to you in the here and now. Say to yourself, "I give myself open space and free time . . . to breathe and enjoy myself."

Because Roger knew he was chronically suffering from constant rushing and time stress, he was a good student. He experimented at work and found that he could gain almost immediate relief once he'd mastered the quick wake-up process.

And the statement "I give myself open space and free time . . . to breathe and enjoy myself" became his at-work mantra that more and more took over his mind. Right in the middle of his hectic workday he discovered that he could expand his awareness to also include a quality of consciousness in which, through all the hustle, he was also giving himself open space to breathe and enjoy himself – every minute!

Of course, especially in the beginning, Roger would often lose his expanded awareness and collapse back into fear-based rushing and heartless relating. But, once he realized he had the power to again pause and attain that expanded quality of awareness, where there was always free space to breathe and enjoy himself, his entire experience at the restaurant shifted.

SET THE WORKFORCE FREE

Once Roger realized that he could create breathing space and relaxation right in the middle of his own work experience, he naturally wanted to do the same for his employees – both to be nice to them and also because by giving them breathing space at work, they'd begin relating with customers with more heart contact and friendship than before.

The key for setting his waiters and staff free while still getting the job at hand done well was found, as always, in the fact that we can expand our awareness and still perform all our mundane duties. In fact, we'll perform our duties better when we're more aware and have emotional space left over for sincere empathy. A waiter who is harried and lost in tensions about what to do next is no fun to have to serve you an expensive meal, after all.

Conversely, a waiter who is efficient and enjoying the moment – aware of his or her breathing, emotions, and body – will be a graceful addition to the dining experience.

When, at the next staff meeting, Roger gave the order that his entire team do a bit of training in breath awareness and learn to make their breathing primary at work and everything else secondary, smiles of humor but also of eagerness flashed around the room. Their boss was giving them permission to enjoy themselves at work, and also offering them training in how to be in an expanded state of awareness on the job. What a deal!

And, what a deal it ended up being for everyone. Waiters were given permission to spend one minute, maybe six or seven breaths, just enjoying the present moment with their clientele at each table. They would actually do their breath meditation right there in action, pausing to feel the air flowing in and out their noses for just a moment before launching into their role of taking orders. And the customers would take deep breaths and relax, too – and everyone suddenly was on the same emotional page, enjoying the present moment together.

The result was that waiters took maybe 5 to 10 percent longer with each table – but tips were larger, and within weeks the restaurant had all its tables filled. Roger considered it a major success – and he tried to make me promise not to tell his competitors about his secret. But this is something that can't be hidden – because everybody in the workforce deserves to be given the freedom to create free breathing space at work.

REGAINING YOUR SOUL

My grandfather was a cattle rancher in early California who was born before the advent of cars and radio and telephone and all the rest. He settled land up a back canyon where there were still a few Chumash Indians living quietly away from the emerging buzz of the new civilization. He learned a lot from these so-called primitives. In fact, much of the wisdom behind what I'm teaching you, my grandfather learned from these people and passed down to me.

> Primary to what my grandfather taught me was the observation that when people go too fast and get fixated on their future responsibilities and projections, they tend to lose their souls and become walking, talking robots without any positive emotional impact at all.

I'm not a reactionary to our present world situation, but there's a certain truth we must be careful to honor – that the faster we buzz in life, the more we lose our present-moment experience through rushing into the future. Everything is constantly speeding up. We've made a god of acceleration. Faster is better.

I feel the necessity to stand up and shout from the rooftops that faster is not necessarily better, especially in our daily business lives. And this is verified psychologically. Yes, we can process data faster and faster in our minds, but the data processing becomes less and less complete the faster we go. And, we can push our bodies fast from meeting to meeting, but we must deal with major stress factors as a result. We can't, however, push such things as the development of a business relationship, nor can we push our emotions to express themselves more speedily.

> One of the greatest mistakes being made by all levels of business
> is the universal tendency to push employees and executives to
> rush absolutely everything in their business routine.

We're approaching the state of the lemmings that rush faster
and faster and end up rushing right off the proverbial cliff. I
remember my granddad getting several tickets on the new free-
way that eventually was built into town – because he was going
too slow! He'd insist before the judge that his soul couldn't go
faster than 35 miles an hour, and that he sure wasn't going to
go any faster than his soul or he'd end up getting to town with
no soul at all. What would be the point of that?

Of course, his story is a bit extreme (although quite true) but
the point is well taken. What's the value of hurrying everyone
in a company so fast that they lose contact with the essential
quality of consciousness that enables them to relate with power
and empathy and conviction and wisdom? What good is an
executive who's so pressured and consumed with future worries and plans that she doesn't have the ability to relate successfully with important clients in the present moment? And, what
value is gained by pressuring a brainstorming team with time
limits to where the creative muse is lost in the process?

What's the value in your own life of letting worries and time
pressures and deadlines and workload push you so quickly and
frenetically into the future that you're barely present in the
here and now, where all real business actually takes place?

And, deeper down, what's the value of your decisions and actions if they're being made in a scattered state of consciousness where you lose touch with your soul, with your sense of right and wrong, with the feelings in your own heart?

When the basic qualities that make us full, responsive human beings are taken away from us, we begin to malfunction. When stress and worries and deadlines collapse our awareness of the present moment, we lose our effectiveness in the present moment. Surely, when examined rationally by reasonable business leaders, it makes no sense at all to run our workforce at such a hectic pace that the underlying performance of the workforce begins to falter – but that's clearly what we're doing. And, because it is bad business practice, the only reason we continue our manic pace at work is through lack of clear awareness of the situation.

THE EMPLOYEE BILL OF RIGHTS

I do believe that, in work as well as anywhere else, we all have the inalienable right to maintain certain qualities of consciousness that make us truly human. We all have the right to enjoy the present moment as it unfolds in our lives. And, we all have the right to stay heart-centered in all that we do. This chapter focuses on the choice and the power that we all have to claim our rights – even in the midst of a hectic Saturday night working in a restaurant and constantly under time pressure. We all have the right to breathe freely and enjoy our work.

The wise manager will realize that by posting an "employee bill of rights" front-center at work, a step is being made in the direction of optimizing employee performance and satisfaction. As we're seeing, especially in this current customer-driven economy where the state of mind of the employee determines the quality of experience of the customer, any step that employers can make to brighten the mood and presence of their employees is good business.

The good news, especially for managers who still have to get the work done, is that the employee bill of rights can be fully granted without losing any productivity at all. When employees are feeling stressed and hassled and chronically under pressure to push faster into the future, they most definitely reach a point where they break down and malfunction and call in on sick leave or otherwise slow down production.

But, when employees are taught how to enjoy the present moment and claim free breathing space even while getting their work done, they feel more refreshed, energized, clear minded, creative, and friendly.

When employees are denied the freedom to enjoy themselves in the present moment, when they feel violated in their souls by being pushed beyond their emotional limits, then an unconscious rebellion gets started against this violation – resulting in all kinds of mostly unconscious worker sabotage that hurts everyone.

But, please don't think I'm just shouting at management here. Most of us are our own worst slave drivers, pushing ourselves even when there's no external pressure.

We set goals beyond our natural limits and force ourselves to try to meet those unrealistic goals. Out of competitive and economic pressures, we struggle to go faster and faster and do more and more – until eventually our bodies and our emotions have had more than enough, and we break down. Either that, or we actually somehow manage to succeed with our extreme career goals, but lose our souls and emotional identities in the process.

I have worked with so many business burnouts that I know this syndrome by heart. Driven by anxieties about money or career and unrealistic visions of luxury and eventual retirement into paradise, so many people sacrifice their enjoyment of the present moment for year after year, striving to reach some future status where, finally, they can pause and enjoy life. Meanwhile, their families suffer, their bodies suffer, their hearts suffer – and even if they attain their goals, they have lost the ability to relax and enjoy life.

This is an all-too-common, very sad story that I hope we can begin to move away from en masse. I'm not saying you have to give up your dreams. I'm just saying don't sacrifice the present moment for them. These are the good old days – enjoy them!

FRIENDSHIP BUBBLE

As we've seen in our discussion thus far, there is a quality of consciousness that exists only in the present moment. In this moment, you breathe and feel and enjoy life, and you also engage with other people at heart levels. There's definitely a direct relationship between insisting on maintaining your basic emotional rights at work and being able to establish heart contact with customers and colleagues.

> Awareness is actually experienced as a bubble of consciousness that you maintain (or fail to maintain) and that surrounds your own physical and emotional presence.

You're aware (hopefully) of your inner feelings and presence right now, for example. If you're maintaining a minimum level of consciousness, you're aware of your breathing as you read these words, and perhaps also certain areas of your body. Hopefully you're also aware of your general emotional mood and feelings in your heart and, in extension, throughout your entire body. Thus, you're aware of the inner bubble that is you.

If you're tuned into your five senses – sight, hearing, touch, smell, and taste – then you're also aware beyond your own body. Your awareness is the sum total of all of the sensory inputs you're integrating from these various sources unified into one sense of being. This is the awareness bubble that you live in, moment to moment, and it's constantly expanding, shifting, contracting, expanding again, and shifting again. This is you, beyond your own mental activity – this is the present-moment self that is created continually through the interaction of your inner world and the outside world.

As you prepare for a business encounter of any kind, you are well advised to pause and notice the condition of your awareness bubble – and to take action to expand this awareness bubble if you find it contracted. We've seen that when you're lost in the past or the future, your bubble of present-moment consciousness is almost nil – you're just not here. We've also seen that when you're rushing too fast and under pressure, your present-moment bubble also collapses.

> When you move into an interpersonal encounter, the person you're meeting with is going to be unable to relate with you unless you are in the present moment of sensory engagement and have created breathing space wherein you have time and emotional space to experience the person.

What actually happens when two people meet is that the separate awareness bubbles come into contact to generate a greater bubble of awareness that includes the two people. I call this the "friendship bubble." Within this greater awareness bubble, the two people share time and space and experience, and thus have the opportunity to make heart contact and become friends.

The wise approach to encouraging this interpersonal experience is to make sure that your personal bubble of awareness is as expanded as possible before a new encounter begins. As we'll see in the following chapters, the moment of encounter can elicit old habits that make your personal awareness bubble contract – so it's best to enter into an encounter with as much awareness as possible.

This chapter is all about maintaining a sense of open space and free time within which friendship can come into being. Following is a clear list of the actions you can take as preparation to make sure there's room for friendship to come into being.

1. Stop hurting: By turning your attention to your breathing experience, you snap out of your mental push into the future and retain the organic sense of your body's own pace, breath by breath, through the unfolding present moment.

2. Start feeling: By also being aware of the feelings in your heart as you breathe, you shift from thought to emotion and further expand your awareness of the world in the here and now.

3. Create free time: By expanding your awareness in the present moment to include good feelings in your body, and also by tuning into the sounds and sights and scents around you, you enter into an awareness of open space and can share space with others.

4. Reclaim your soul: By insisting on the freedom to enjoy the present moment, you relax and tap into the genuine feelings in your heart and expand your awareness bubble to fill the space around you.

By moving through these four basic steps, which are drawn from what you've learned thus far, you prepare yourself for a positive encounter with whomever you're meeting. Naturally, if you're at work in any capacity, you have a role to play and a job to further. At the same time, you've gone beyond your formal job description and shifted into the quality of consciousness that makes genuine relating possible.

When Nothing Works

Thus far in this book, we've been quite positive and assumed that you can move fairly easily through the various techniques being explored. For most of you, some of the time, this will be true – these are methods that do work and that most people can readily master with a bit of discipline.

However, some of you are going to find that you sometimes sink into dark moods where nothing helps – you're just stuck there and can hardly find your breathing at all, let alone your heart. Either that, or your heart is in such emotional pain and torment, or so cold and distant, that you just can't focus there at all. What to do?

Short-Term Advice

When you begin to move through this basic Listening with Empathy process but find that you are stuck in a negative mood such as anxiety, depression, confusion, or anger, hold in mind that sometimes you simply must ride out a mood. Time must go by before some deep, inner process sets you free from the grip of a buried one-liner that's so old and ingrained that more positive focus phrases don't dispel it.

Let me be totally honest here. I personally sink into a rather bothersome depression for two to three hours about once or sometimes twice a month. I don't know why – but I know that if I struggle against the depression, it only gets worse. Sure, I have a bunch of pet theories for its cause. And, it happens less and less in my life the more I exercise my ability to shift moods at will. But it's still there sometimes, and it's a part of me.

So again, I use emotional judo. I accept myself just as I am rather than deny the depression. I give myself permission to feel good over and over, just to remind myself of the direction I want to move in. And, I stay as aware of my breathing and even those agonizing feelings in my heart as I can. This is to say, I keep moving through the basic set of focus phrases, even if it looks like they aren't doing me any good this time.

And, sure enough, at some point I hear the words I'm saying, feel the cloud lifts, and I'm okay again. I can expand my awareness and enjoy the present moment. I share this with you because I want it clear that I'm not offering some magical escape from occasional bouts of unwanted emotions.

In general, my techniques will help you greatly and will move you into a more enjoyable present moment throughout your day. But, sometimes life is hard and we struggle and suffer emotionally. That's part of the life experience, too.

So, do all you can from the inside out, using these methods

to brighten your mood and lift your load. Be sure to also go online to www.listeningwithempathy.com and take advantage of all the various programs I've developed for different emotional problems and their realistic cures. You can do a great deal on your own to improve your emotional condition!

Long-Term Advice

What do you do when nothing seems to work and you continue to suffer emotionally? If you explore the method taught in this book and all the emotional healing programs I offer online, and still you find that you're having your work life disturbed by unwanted emotions and attitudes, I do recommend that rather than suffering any more that you seek support groups and professional help to actively deal with your condition.

For instance, many people find remarkable aid from joining a regular biweekly yoga class, a dance group, or a gym where you can work out and blow off steam through exercise. A fulfilling hobby often helps a great deal. And, when you feel seriously in need, consult a cognitive therapist who can work with you using the basic principles common to my methods, but focused specifically on your particular needs. It's an act of courage and hope to seek out such help!

Through it all, I can't overstate the importance of continuing to learn how to take charge of your mind, make conscious choices about how you manage your moods, and assume as much responsibility as you can – each new day for the rest of your life – for your own inner experience.

You'll find that managing your thoughts and moods improves your performance at work, increases your empathy quotient, and helps you succeed in your relationships. This inner consciousness work will also help you make contact with your spiritual core of being and wake up realms of experience that truly make life an infinite journey of discovery.

BEYOND PREPARATION

To end this first section of our book, let's see how you're doing and how you feel about advancing to the next step of our program, that of shifting from preparation . . . into that crucial moment of encounter.

Whether you've had ten seconds or five minutes to prepare for a sales meeting or whatever other situation that brings you together with another person in a business setting, at some point the preparation period comes to an end and the action period of empathic engagement begins. You've had your chance to get ready – how good a job did you do?

When you first begin working with this Listening with Empathy method, of course you're not going to instantly shift totally in the desired direction. Just like learning any other activity or procedure, practice is what makes perfect.

Right here at the beginning of your training, please burn into your memory the order of importance and proper sequence of the various steps you're in the process of memorizing. If you know the first step, the other steps can be added one by one.

What is that first step that you will always want to make, given one breath or ten minutes for preparation for an encounter? I'm not going to tell you. Rather, I want you to remember for yourself where to turn your mind's attention right now as the beginning of the process of expanding your awareness bubble. What's that constant available experience that's always there waiting for you to turn your attention toward it? What's that sensory phenomenon happening right under your own nose right now that can instantly wake up your awareness of your own presence?

And, once you tune into your breath anchor, the next step is so organic you don't have to think about it – you just allow your awareness to expand so that you're aware of both the air flowing in and out of your nose and the movements in your chest and belly as you breathe. It's all one process, and you can be aware of it all at once. And, when you're aware of your full breath experience in the present moment, quite naturally your thoughts become quiet because the past and the future temporarily let go their grip on your mind.

And then, of course, the next expansion is easy, whether or not you say the focus phrase that encourages the expansion – to include the feelings in your heart, right in the middle of your breathing experience. Once you get good at this, the entire

process will happen very rapidly as you stop fixating on individual points and take in the whole at once.

Likewise, the next expansion is logical and effortless – to expand your awareness to include your whole body here in the present moment, feeling good, tuned into all the sensory happenings all around you, and expanding your bubble so that you're a bright presence as you now go into action and encounter the person you're meeting with!

Following is the short-order presentation of the preparation process you're learning. Please begin to memorize this set of focus phrases. Also feel free to use our online training for further guidance and effortless learning – make this process a new permanent habit!

PROGRAM REVIEW

PHASE 1: PREPARING FOR AN ENCOUNTER

Quick Review

Before meeting with a customer, client, or colleague, it's vital to employ an effective cognitive-shifting method to put aside any inner stress, worries, or judgments that pollute an encounter – and shift your focus toward positive feelings and heart-centered emotions. You can accomplish this in just one to two minutes.

Key Focus Phrases

1. "I feel the air flowing in and out of my nose . . ."

2. "I also feel the movements in my chest and belly . . ."

3. "I'm also aware of the feelings in my heart . . ."

4. "I give myself permission to feel good . . ."

5. "My mind is quiet, my emotions calm . . ."

6. "I honor and respect the person I'm meeting with . . ."

7. "I feel good toward my own self . . ."

8. "I'm ready to be friendly and cheerful, to listen without manipulation, and to help satisfy this person's needs . . ."

Points to Remember

Before an encounter, always remember to act on the four primary choices that brighten your empathy charge:

1. Focus on . . . the present moment: When your

attention is gone from the present moment, you're not really aware of the customer at all – and not available for genuine relating. Therefore, the first step you always need to take is to shift fully into the present moment – where all experience and relating take place.

2: Focus on . . . your heart: Most people tend to stay fixated on the thoughts and images, memories and imaginations constantly running through their minds. Customers pick up this lack of warmth and react to it. Therefore, before an encounter with a client, customer, or any other significant person, it's essential to shift your attention from head to heart.

3: Focus on . . . feeling good: If we're feeling bad, we're not going to help clients and customers feel good. Therefore, in preparation for a business or social encounter, it's essential to consciously choose to shift from feeling bad to feeling good.

4: Focus on . . . your positive intent: If your habitual intent is to manipulate a customer rather than help that person get what they need, your empathy quotient will drop very low and the customer will react negatively. Therefore, it's important that you consciously state a clear, positive intent before a sales or service engagement so that you aim your focus of intent directly where it will best serve you.

Reflection Time

For each of the four sections of this book, I would like to offer you a page or two of questions that will lead you into deep reflection and inner contemplation. I recommend that you turn to these pages a number of times during the next weeks and months – to stimulate personal insight and ongoing emotional and attitudinal growth. Ultimately, you're the one running your power of attention – I'm here to recommend pointing your attention in rewarding directions. So take a bit of time, stay aware of your breathing and your heart . . . and ask yourself:

1. In your past, would you say that you have been mostly fair in business, honestly serving your clients and customers?

2. Does it feel more gratifying within your heart to take advantage of someone in business and make a big score, or to make sure they benefit as much as you do?

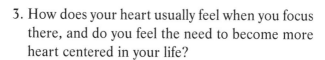
3. How does your heart usually feel when you focus there, and do you feel the need to become more heart centered in your life?

4. What do you tend to worry about, day in and day out – and are you ready to finally let go of the habit of worrying?

5. What does it mean to stop judging people, and to accept them as they are? Is this possible; and what will happen if you do this?

6. What does it feel like, to open your heart to receive friendship – is there a danger in doing this? And how do you actually do this?

AUDIO SCRIPT: CLASS ONE

Go to www.listeningwithempathy.com for audio guidance.

Imagine that in a few moments you have a phone call or a conference scheduled or you're meeting with a client or a customer is going to walk in the door. What can you do rapidly to shift into optimum mental and emotional condition for positive relating and emotional bonding?

First of all, be sure to turn your attention to your breathing – notice if your breathing is relaxed and enjoyable, or tight and tense . . . and say to yourself, "I give myself permission to feel good."

Feel the air flowing in and out of your nose . . . relax your tongue and jaw . . . let your eye muscles and face muscles relax . . . expand your awareness to include the movements in your chest and belly . . . move your pelvis a bit as you breathe . . . tap into your power deep in your belly . . . and say to yourself, "I let go of my worries and feel peaceful inside."

Now expand your awareness to include the feelings in your heart . . . wake up your center of empathy . . . and say to yourself, "I accept the person I'm meeting . . . I open my heart to this person."

In this expanded quality of consciousness, as you enter into your encounter with this person, be sure to hold your primary focus on your own breathing, your own power, your own heartfelt warmth and acceptance . . . and if you have a bit more time, also say to yourself:

"I want to listen to this person's needs,"

"I want to help this person satisfy their needs,"

"I want to make a new friend."

And with this full preparation and positive intent, you can now go confidently into action. Just enjoy yourself and let your bright mood raise your client's mood – and they'll want to spend time with you again.

The Moment of Encounter

CHAPTER 4

MAINTAIN YOUR INNER FOCUS

We know that the impression we create during the first moments of meeting someone is vital to the success of that meeting. But, we all have our own set of preprogrammed routines that we tend to lock into when we meet someone – routines that don't necessarily serve us well at all. Perhaps we know this person already. Perhaps it's our first meeting. We might be in a retail storefront meeting a casual customer, or encountering the head of our company. Perhaps we're getting together with a repeat client or even nervously shaking hands with the prime minister.

Regardless of the particulars of the situation, there's almost always a momentary emotional challenge where we tend to go partly unconscious, operate on social automatic – and at least partly lose heartfelt contact and emotional warmth.

THE MOMENT OF ENCOUNTER

If you're like me and the majority of our population, when you were a child you probably fell victim to feelings of shyness, confusion, and embarrassment when forced to meet someone you didn't know. As children, almost everyone developed reflexive habits of physical tension and emotional contraction that would come into play at the moment of an encounter. And, these old habits tend to carry through into our adult lives unless we consciously act to transcend them. This chapter is all about that process of consciously overriding old encounter habits so that the moment of encounter stays relaxed, engaging, and genuinely friendly.

FOUR DEFENSE PLOYS

Different people develop different façades to help hide their momentary shyness or awkwardness during the first moments of an encounter. George, for instance, the extroverted salesman from our first chapter, had the rather bothersome habit of overpowering the other person with his dominating presence, throwing pre-canned comments rapidly at the person so that, rather than showing his natural shyness and vulnerability, George came across as invulnerable and immune to what he considered weak emotions.

The result of George's defensive mechanisms was an instant contraction on the part of the other person, who felt almost attacked by George's supposed show of enthusiasm and friendliness.

George left zero room for open space and free time to get a feel for the other person. He barely took in the other person's presence at all. Instead, he would push the meeting with a jolt into a conversation game that he entirely dominated, like a tennis player immediately rushing to net and slamming every return down the other person's throat.

Karen, the moody executive we met in chapter two, would do just the opposite. She hated phoniness and instead wore her emotions on her sleeve, forcing the other person to accept whatever mood she might be in as if the most important thing at that moment were her personal feelings. When she was in a good mood, all went well. She was warm and open and sensitive to the other person's needs and feelings. But, when she was in a hostile mood or sulking or caught in a bout of anxiety, the other person got a full dose of these negative moods, like it or not.

Karen also too often filled the "breathing space" in the room with her emotional presence so that the other person didn't really have room to relax and enjoy the present moment. People like Karen actually cause others' breathing to tighten and become shallow as if there isn't enough air for both to breathe in the room – or, as if the other person doesn't want to breathe in such negative emotional vibes.

In this way, Karen was like George. They both used up all the consciousness space in the room, leaving the other person almost literally gasping for air and eager to get out of the room.

THE MOMENT OF ENCOUNTER

Perhaps I'm exaggerating a bit with these examples because sometimes both of these people happened to be in a particularly relaxed, friendly mood to begin with and they would succeed in granting the other person breathing space and making genuine heart contact. Neither of them was so extreme that they regularly malfunctioned, or they would have lost their jobs long ago. But, both of them definitely had the tendency to dominate another person's breathing space and evoke contracted emotions rather than genuinely friendly ones.

Roger, from our third chapter, did just the opposite – he knew how to control his emotions and be a suave conversationalist. But, because he wasn't really present at all, gone from the here and now with his mind focused on a dozen problems back in the kitchen, he left the people he encountered in an emotional vacuum. He was there talking to them and demanding their attention and expecting them to play his conversational game – but their emotional feeling was that of being ignored, hardly noticed at all.

A fourth common reaction to the encounter situation is plain old bashfulness and a freezing of social graces – you know the feeling. Your mind suddenly goes blank, you are hardly aware at all (the result of temporary social anxiety), and you get all caught up in your own nervousness so that it's difficult to make contact and socialize. The "moment of encounter" technique I'm going to teach you in this chapter will help you with any or all four of the above reactions.

STAYING ANCHORED

Thus far, we seem to have spent a long time learning to master a remarkably (or so it seemed) simple focusing process – that of turning your attention to your breathing and not losing that focus even when you are doing other things. We've seen that if you want to hold your attention in the present moment (which is essential for a successful encounter), you simply must stay aware of your breathing as your awareness anchor.

> But, as soon as you are confronted with a challenging situation, what often happens is that you suddenly contract your awareness and lose that crucial breath anchor that links you to your own emotions.

That's why over and over I keep saying that you must make your awareness of your breathing primary and all other things secondary. When you're aware of your breathing, for example, you're conscious of the air flowing in and out of your nose, which directly connects you with the air around you that you're breathing – which instantly and organically connects you with the air the other person is breathing.

Right at the moment of encounter with another person, the primary thing you have in common is that you're both breathing from the same sea of air that surrounds you. The atmosphere itself is the genuine link that enables the two of you to be together – and to stay aware of this foundation reality is to make sure you feel connected at primal levels with the person.

After all, when you speak, you broadcast your inner emotions and thoughts through the air and into the other person's ears and awareness. The air is your communication medium. Likewise, with the powerful sensory connection of seeing each other – this happens within the atmospheric sea as well.

What I'm saying here is that if you want to make sure you stay aware of and in touch with a person you're meeting, you must stay aware of the space you're suddenly sharing. And, the proven best way to do this is simply to make sure you remain aware of the air flowing in and out of your nose – that's just the reality of a successful encounter.

> This breath anchor does something else vital as well. It leads you deep inside yourself with each inhale, right into your lungs – which happen to surround your heart.

This is why I've also made a major point of teaching how to expand your awareness to include both your breathing experience and also your emotional experience right in the middle of your breathing. In fact, if you pause to reflect a moment, you'll realize that your primary vehicle for expressing your inner feelings with another person, besides movement of your body, is vocalization. What is vocalization? Nothing more than a particular employment of that breathing experience that you're aware of: each new inhale and exhale.

When you come together with someone, usually you're going to begin talking to this person fairly soon. What I'm suggesting is that you make sure the words you express

THE MOMENT OF ENCOUNTER

come consciously from that awareness of your breathing and your inner feelings. Then you are fairly certain to make heart contact through your voice – because you have your voice consciously connected through your awareness, with your inner feelings in your heart. So, stay anchored in your breath – that's the key!

HARD SCIENTIFIC EVIDENCE

What actually happens energetically when two people come together? Certainly there is sensory stimulation in both directions, where you see and hear each other and maybe smell each other. If you shake hands or exchange a hug, you also feel each other's presence for a moment. All of these inputs can communicate subtle (or even obvious) information about your emotional feelings toward the other person and your general stance in the meeting.

But, we now know scientifically that there are other definite factors to consider when two people, two biological organisms, come together.

First of all, experimental instruments can now detect a definite, complex, electromagnetic broadcast that surrounds your body and radiates outward in all directions at least 15 feet. It is generated primarily by your heart and spinal column. When you are in an angry mood, this broadcast has a

THE MOMENT OF ENCOUNTER

particular configuration that strikes the other person's nervous system and impacts their energetic condition. If you're feeling sad, this emotion is broadcasted, as well as all other emotional conditions.

This means that you can't really hide your emotions from a person through clever behavior and conversation. You're hitting this person directly at this electromagnetic level from the moment you enter the room and approach the person (go to www.listeningwithempathy.com for documentation of this research). Likewise, you're receiving whatever electromagnetic broadcast the other person is sending out into the world. The two of you are exchanging emotional information even if you don't consciously take note of it – you're affecting each other.

> This is one of the reasons why preparation for an encounter is so important – so that you can consciously say focus phrases that break your mind out of the ruminations and chronic thoughts that, in turn, generate the energetic condition in your body.

So to whatever extent you can find a few moments before an encounter, it's vastly to your advantage to take responsibility for the emotional charge you're packing and to do what you can to shift into a more positive state of mind and body.

Not only do you broadcast your heart's general condition out into the world, ten years of very fine experimentation at

PEAR (mentioned earlier) have proven beyond a scientific doubt that your brain also broadcasts an as-yet undefined power out into the physical world that has the capacity to alter the functioning of a sensitive machine and also to influence the thoughts of another person. In literally tens of thousands of test runs with hundreds of different subjects, the statistical results proved that a person's power of intent can influence the performance of a random-number generator – not with overly large results, but definitely with statistically significant results based on universal experimental models. You can go to my website for this research verification or directly to www.princeton.edu/~pear.

This research has caused great confusion in traditional scientific circles because it proves what so many people have always claimed intuitively – that the mind does have power over matter. Specifically, one person's thoughts can be received by another person's mind. The effect is certainly subtle, but it's scientifically verifiable and should be dealt with from here on out.

This is why you can be full of great talk and convincing arguments, but if your own mind is projecting different thoughts, then the person you're relating with is going to receive these thought projections and react accordingly. George admitted that he often was holding the thought, "Boy, this guy is really easy to manipulate," even while his expression and words were being friendly and soothing.

As soon as George learned about the Princeton studies, he began to take responsibility for his attitudes and thoughts during an encounter so that he wasn't subtly poisoning his business and personal relationships.

For the record, the Princeton studies also showed that the thoughts you think about someone project a great distance, and even seem to linger so that they can be picked up at a later time by the other person. So, let go of the idea that your negative thoughts and judgments don't influence people at a distance and in the future.

The negative side of all this research is staggering because it means that all of your negative thoughts and emotions are constantly affecting the world around you, creating damage even when you're not with the other person. The good news is that you can positively influence an encounter not only when you're with the person, but both before and after the meeting.

Suddenly you see the added power of pausing before an encounter and saying to yourself, "I accept this person I'm going to meet with just as they are." The words help shift your inner feelings in that accepting direction and even right then before you meet, the person has been positively affected by your thoughts and feelings. Now you see just how powerful your preparation time can be!

SHARING SPACE AND TIME

Once you realize how much is happening when you meet with someone, the notion of sharing time and space with this person becomes especially exciting. If you're not taking responsibility for all the different variables of the encounter, surely you're in danger of having an unsuccessful meeting – even though you didn't mean to. Conversely, once you begin to realize all the variables you have at your disposal to guarantee that the meeting goes well, you can relax and feel more in charge of the encounter.

> Key to all of this is making sure that you do what I taught Roger to do – relax, focus on the present moment, and simply share time and space with another person.

If you don't do this, then you can't really make heart contact with them. And if you don't make heart contact with them, then no friendship and sense of bonding or loyalty can develop. That's the psychological reality we're dealing with here.

When you're locked up in your thoughts, there's in a very real sense no space or time at all to experience and share. As cognitive science explains, abstract thoughts take place in a two-dimensional, linear reality. There's no depth or volume to a thought, after all. It's simply a flow of words and images and symbols through your mind. That's why you can get lost in thought and not know where you are or how much time has

transpired – you've been gone from the three-dimensional space/time experience.

So, if you want to share time and space with someone, you simply must temporarily shut down your inner fixation on thoughts and plans and future projections and all the rest. You must actively create space and time within which to relate. You do this by tuning into your breathing and then expanding your awareness back into three-dimensional reality by also being aware of the expanding and contracting volume inside your chest and belly. You actually create space and time!

> It's so simple and organic and basic – but if you don't do it, you're not going to be able to experience the three-dimensional presence of the person you're with. I hope this is clear.

The proof is in your own experience. Whenever you're lost in thought, notice what happens when you again return your focus of attention to the air flowing in and out of your nose (do it now!) and then expand your awareness to include the volume inside your chest and belly – and pop! Here you are again. Go the next step and include the feelings in your heart. You're now ready to express your feelings through your voice on your exhales and to broadcast on all fronts so that the other person actually feels your presence, mood, and intent via all of these various inputs we've been talking about.

ACTUALLY DOING IT

I know that this chapter is an intense one. I've just discussed in 12 pages what usually takes 50 pages – but I think you'll "get it" perhaps even better in this particular framework and in the context of the dynamics of a business encounter. So let's move right into my recommendation of what to actually do at these engagement levels. Naturally, you're going to need practice mastering this crucial part of a successful encounter. Give yourself time, play with this process, and don't be upset when you slip back into your old habits. Just keep returning to the process and moving through it again.

Preparation: First of all, take very seriously what you've learned about and begun to master in the first three chapters. The preparation time is half the story of successfully encountering someone. So, begin to create a bit more free time before a meeting so that you can move through the full two-minute process.

Breath anchor: And then, when you go into action and come face to face with someone, train yourself to remain aware of your breathing, the air flowing in and out of your nose or mouth (sometimes you breathe through your mouth, not your nose – no dif-

ference). If that's all you can do during a meeting, then that's enough for now. Practice all the time, all day at work and also with your family and friends after work. Get better and better at staying aware of your breathing, and all that implies, when you're relating with people.

Sharing space: When you can, expand your awareness to include the air around you, the space and volume that you're sharing with this person. Be aware that you're both breathing from the same shared air supply. Let this shared medium further bond the two of you. Notice that when you're aware of your inhales and exhales, you tap into an organic sense of time going by. You become aware through your breathing rhythm of sharing time – and within this shared sense of time and space, you can make genuine emotional contact in the here and now.

That's a lot to do in the first moments of an encounter. We'll return in later chapters to talk about how to deepen the sense of contact with the person. For now, just hold as primary your awareness of your own inner presence because without that awareness of your own presence there's really no one present for the other person to relate with.

CHAPTER 5

DON'T SLIP INTO JUDGMENT

Let's now take a close look at what defines and influences the experience of the person you're meeting with. The term "customer experience" is used very loosely. What are the psychological reality and variables of customer experience?

As mentioned, a customer's experience is definitely affected by the physical environment and ambiance of your office, store, restaurant, home, or wherever you've chosen to meet. This variable does need to be considered, and modified if necessary to present a comfortable and welcoming atmosphere for your meeting. But, it's important not to try to over-impress the person.

On all fronts, customers are sensitive to phoniness. Being who you naturally are in an environment that honestly reflects your product or service will evoke the most positive experience in the client.

First impressions are, indeed, very important. The customer is going to quickly survey your physical environment and make snap judgments based on the visual surroundings you maintain, which represent you and your product or service. It's obvious that if your environment is a mess, your service will probably be the same – and the customer will react.

At bottom, a customer's experience is the sum total of all the sensory inputs that are received during your meeting, combined with all the thoughts and moods and bodily conditions that the customer brings to the meeting. Your hope is that your environment – and your own presence, mood, and behavior – will positively impact the inner experience of the customer, raising this person's mood and making them feel better.

And, naturally, the main focus of the customer is liable to be on you – how you dress and move and feel and talk, and how your more subtle emotional presence generates reactions and judgments within the customer's inner experience.

The initial perception a client receives of who you are will strongly influence the outcome of the meeting. And that perception happens mostly on subconscious, perceptual levels. What are the primary judgments that most people make in a meeting?

DANGER

We are programmed to look first to see if the situation we've entered carries any signs of danger. George, for instance, would come lumbering fast toward a client and make a show of his strength – and instantly make women in particular react with fear, even though that wasn't his intention. Karen's various moods would push related danger buttons in her encounters. When she was feeling anxious, the other person would subconsciously tense up in anticipation of danger. When Karen was feeling aggressive, the other person would feel threatened.

If you want to assure someone that you're not a threat, the very best way to do this is in your preparation time. Go through the focus phrases one by one and look to see if you're feeling anxious, judgmental, or aggressive. And, saying the focus phrases, you will shift in the direction of feeling calm, confident, and accepting. Your feelings are what impact a person the most, and those are variables you're now learning to control. The last thing you want to do is make someone feel somehow threatened, insecure, or in danger.

Your movements themselves will be a primary indicator of whether you're a danger. When you're not aware of your own body, you're liable to make movements that might appear threatening. But, when you're aware of your movements in the present moment, you become graceful, you're in charge of your body – and that's a primary indicator that you're safe to spend time with. Also, when you're aware of the other person's physical presence, you'll move with respect in that person's personal territory and not inadvertently violate it. Again, awareness is the key to success.

THE MOMENT OF ENCOUNTER

INTEREST

Once a person is sure they can relax and not worry about danger of any kind, they usually want to know if anyone is paying attention to them or if they're being ignored. We've seen already that if you are lost in thoughts about the past or the future, the other person will feel ignored because they don't feel your attention focused on them. Therefore, it's vital to make sure at that moment of encounter that your full attention is devoted to the present moment.

However, this doesn't mean totally fixating on your perception of the other person. Too many people make the mistake of thinking that if they give someone their full attention, this indicates strong interest. But, if you don't retain at least part of your mind's awareness to focus on your own self, there's basically "nobody at home" in your own body and the other person can't feel your presence at all. Because many people (like George in the old days) use "total attention" to hide their own lack of genuine interest in another person, many customers are highly sensitive to being overpowered with too much attention.

Instead, practice until you perfect the fine art of expanding your awareness so that you're fully aware of the other person's presence in the room, and at the same time fully aware of your own presence in the room. This is truly the hinge point of the ultimate art of successful relating – inner and outer awareness at the same time. And, again, the key is holding your attention to your breathing devotedly and at the same time opening your heart to be truly receptive to the other person's presence.

> We've seen earlier in this chapter that being receptive to another person's presence means not only listening and looking in their direction, but also being receptive to projections of their heart and mind.

This is not an "out there" notion. The electromagnetic broadcast from a customer's heart region can be registered on scientific dials. If you want to pick up the heart-centered feelings of another person, the psychological process requires that you tune into your own heart and notice what feelings you pick up from the other person. Sensitive people, especially women, for centuries have been talking about being able to directly sense the feelings of those around them. Now, we know that this is possible – and you can begin developing your ability to tune into your heart and listen to what it has to say at subtle levels about the person with you.

INTERACTION

As we're seeing, when two people come together and focus upon each other, many levels of interaction are possible. You see each other and respond to each other's movements and facial expressions. You talk to each other and share your ideas and intents. You might touch, shake hands or hug, and feel each other's physical presence. And, yes, your heart and brain projections actually impact each other at subtle levels.

There's even another level of subtle interaction to consider. I've seen demonstrations of how two electromagnetic force fields alter each other's configurations – and generate a third unified, energetic expression. When two people come together, their mental and electromagnetic force fields influence each other and generate a unified presence in the room that represents the merger of both into one greater energetic presence. This sounds like science fiction to be sure, but it is now proven to be a subtle reality that we are all involved in every time we come together with another person.

> The key factors for maximizing this deep sense of bonding are awareness, receptivity, and trust.

If you are not aware of your own presence in the here and now, you won't experience at this level. If you're not tuned into your heart and open to be affected by the other person, you won't experience the bonding experience. And, if you don't trust this other person, then your defensiveness will counteract their possible openness to heart contact.

We are now at the core of what is called "customer bonding" – that actual experience of opening up, sharing time and space, and being somehow influenced by the other person. In a very real and energetic way, your two hearts and your separate feelings and thoughts merge, and you experience that great feeling of truly "being together" with another human being. This experience feels very good – and it's the crux of the customer-bonding issue.

TRUST AND RESPECT

There's a final dimension to talk about in this regard – whether you trust this other person without any anxiety and perceive them without judgment as an equal – or if your mind and emotions are judging the person negatively and thus creating friction between the two of you.

We talked a bit about trust and judgment in chapter two, where you learned the focus phrase "I accept the person I'm meeting with just as they are." I threw that potent statement at you fast and moved on – now it's time to pause and look more closely at this important variable in an encounter. Nobody likes feeling judged. Everybody likes feeling accepted just as they are, but most of us are diehard, compulsive judgers.

Judging is a natural function of the mind. We are constantly looking or listening or tasting or touching, and then instantly making judgments about what our senses are picking up in our environment. Judging whether or not something is dangerous, bad, unhealthy, boring, bothersome, or otherwise to be avoided is clearly a necessary part of life. We do best to gravitate toward what we enjoy and is good for us and interesting, and steer clear of what will damage us or waste our time and money.

The problem isn't that we judge – the problem is that we are stuck in judgment gear almost all of the time.

Judgment is essentially a fear-based function of the mind and, as such, it's antithetical to feeling, trusting, accepting, and being friendly. In fact, many psychologists (myself included) have observed that people can't judge and love at the same time. You can't stand back from someone and question their value or safety and at the same time open up to them and enjoy their company. You're either in judgment mode or acceptance mode. And, because your heart is basically shut down when you're judging, the other person is going to feel this closed, defensive, negative stance you're holding and react to it.

So, your challenge right when you encounter someone is to make sure that you are not slipping in judgment mode. How do you do this?

Certainly, hold in your mind the focus phrase "I accept this person just as they are" and remember that judgments are thought-based, associative functions of the mind – so if you want to instantly turn off your judging process, all you need to do is shift your focus of attention away from your thoughts and to what you're experiencing in the here and now. This is to say, quiet your mind by focusing on your breathing experience, your heart experience, and your whole-body experience in the present moment.

Respect emerges from this process as well. When you actively turn off your judgmental mode, you're in effect saying

THE MOMENT OF ENCOUNTER

to this person, "Okay, I respect who you are. I don't need to be careful or to constantly judge your looks and behavior. I trust you and am open to relating with you as an equal. You accept me, I accept you. Let's relate."

TRUST YOURSELF, TOO

You'll find that it works miracles to stop judging the person you're meeting with and accept them just as they are. Suddenly they feel accepted and respected – they can relax and not put on a show or defend themselves. They can enjoy that special heart feeling of being liked for who they are.

But, you short-circuit the heart-to-heart exchange if you're still judging yourself. In fact, it's important to deal with your self-judgment habits first. As the world's great religions all point out, you can't respect and love someone else more than you love yourself. The beginning point of genuine trust and respect and empathy is always your relationship with yourself.

> If you don't honor and trust and accept yourself, no one will be able to honor and trust and accept you – the basic empathic interplay between you and other people will be blocked.

This is why, right after I have you state "I accept the person I'm meeting with just as they are," I also have you turn to the feelings in your heart toward yourself, and say the crucial focus phrase "I honor and accept and love myself just as I am."

THE MOMENT OF ENCOUNTER

The trouble is, most people just – don't. We live in a society where everyone is constantly judging themselves as inadequate. We're not smart enough or handsome enough or fast enough, we're too fat or too skinny, we're not successful enough, or we're not good enough in bed – we're continually hitting ourselves over the head with self-judgment and, as a result, we feel terrible emotionally. And because of this, we don't perform well – and we mistake this as verification that we're not good enough, that we're not lovable, that we're somehow just inadequate. Either that or we puff ourselves up like George used to and try to convince ourselves and others that we're absolutely perfect and magnificent.

After 30-plus years of working with people as a therapist and coach, I can say quite definitely that self-judgment is the primary killer of good times, success, positive relationships, and everything else we hunger for. I know that I'm succeeding with a client when they begin to just ease up on themselves and, rather than trying to change themselves in order to accept themselves, they simply go ahead and accept and love themselves just as they are.

Suddenly, through the power of self-acceptance and love, they then begin to let go of their emotional contractions and negative mental habits – not through denying who they are, but through embracing who they are. It seems like a paradox, but it's true – if you want to change for the better, you must accept yourself just as you are. Then you naturally begin self-correcting and healing emotionally because the power of love is, indeed, the power that heals and enables us to become more fully who we really are.

You can't change who you are. All you can realistically do is accept yourself, and then allow your natural potential to emerge and express itself step by step.

And, meanwhile along the way, as soon as you stop judging yourself and relax into being who you are, your heart feels better, your mind thinks positive thoughts, and you broadcast a presence that is accepting and loving. And bang – customers enjoy sharing time and space with you. At heart, it's that simple. Say it – do it! "I honor and accept and love myself, just as I am." Then it's easy to return to saying "I accept the person I'm meeting with just as they are." In this spirit, the two of you can come together and truly relate and enjoy each other's company. That's what friendship is all about – acceptance and trust.

ALL THINGS IN MODERATION

Having made such strong statements about the negative sides of being in judgment mode in a meeting, let me bring this all back into balance by stating that, of course, a certain amount of judging might be necessary and valuable when you begin a business meeting. From the point of view of empathy and bonding, yes, turn off your judgment mode and give the other person the benefit of the doubt. Enjoy being with them without getting lost in judgmental thoughts about them.

But, at the same time, obviously it's wise, with some people, to momentarily assess if indeed this person is dangerous, on drugs, or somehow just outside the boundaries of full acceptance in the present situation.

> As we'll see later, it's also wise to notice if the person is caught up in their own negative judgments, attitudes, and moods so that you can deal appropriately with their condition and perhaps help move the encounter in more positive directions.

What I'm advocating is that, in general, you do your best to give the other person the benefit of the doubt. Make your predominant emotion that of acceptance and willingness to enjoy sharing space and time. Even if the other person seems in judgment mode against you, you will do best to present a genuine willingness to be accepting. If you hit back with your own judgments, then the meeting will head strongly in negative directions. Be the first to open up and risk a little and see if your readiness to trust and enjoy the moment will positively influence the other person's feelings and thoughts.

And, hold this as a final thought for this chapter – if you stay aware of your breathing, you're going to be in optimum awareness position to respond appropriately to whatever moods and actions the other person brings to the meeting. You'll be spontaneous – and this sense of confident, positive responsiveness to the present moment will enable you to enjoy yourself and participate positively with the other person. That's the stance that will always serve you best – stay positive, enjoy yourself, and see the best in the other person.

THE MOMENT OF ENCOUNTER

CHAPTER   6

LEAD WITH SPONTANEITY

For many of you, this chapter will be the most important thus far because we're going to jump into an exploration of perhaps your most prized yet least understood psychological potential – your ability to be spontaneous at work. You surely know the general feeling of being spontaneous. It's that "in the zone" whole-body quality of consciousness in which you are entirely focused on the unfolding present moment and participating with your whole heart and soul in that unfolding. You're "on" both intellectually and emotionally, and physically as well, and you inherently trust your spontaneous actions because they're emerging from a highly conscious mental function.

When you're acting truly spontaneously, you're functioning in an expanded state of consciousness where the full integrative power of your mind is engaged with what's happening around you.

In this highly alert and responsive state, your awareness is at maximum expansion so that you're processing all of the various sensory inputs coming at you from your environment, and responding without hesitation through the sharpness of your integrated mind. Also, you're not feeling any fear at all. There's no worrying going on in your mind, no anxiety to cloud your thoughts and tense your body and contract your emotional expression. You're simultaneously relaxed and energized, a great listener, and able to express your thoughts and feelings honestly and fully.

And, perhaps most importantly, you're centered in your heart. You're accepting and compassionate and able to open up and share deep, empathic feelings with those around you. You're conscious of all the more subtle inputs being broadcasted by others in the room, and you're also fully tuned into a deep quality of emotional honesty at your own center.

That's my spontaneous definition of spontaneity. It's linguistic origins are from the Latin term *sponte,* of one's free will. It means rising from a momentary impulse; developing without apparent external influence, force, cause, or treatment.

Clearly, in the context of our present discussion on how to be more genuine and empathic emotionally during a business encounter, being spontaneous seems to be a key goal.

THE MOMENT OF ENCOUNTER

There are, of course, numerous pitfalls on the road to effective spontaneity, which we'll discuss in this chapter. But, in general, if you want to succeed with your meeting, being spontaneous is a definite plus.

TRUE OR FALSE

Even though, by definition, being spontaneous seems to be an ideal state of mind from which to operate, there are many culturally conditioned apprehensions that arise when most of us even think about perhaps being more spontaneous at work. Let's look at each of these negative assumptions and see if they're psychologically true or not.

First of all, there's the assumption that if you're spontaneous, you're operating out of control and without adequate reflection and, therefore, in danger of doing something stupid or downright damaging. It's true that when a lot of people begin to "let go" and act spontaneously, they suddenly begin to vent all of their wild, irrational impulses with total disregard for consequences – and often make fools of themselves. However, remember that the definition of spontaneity doesn't include venting irrational impulses at all.

When you're truly spontaneous, you're deeply tuned into your inner sense of right and wrong, of wise and foolish, of trustworthy and dangerous.

The whole point of shifting into a more spontaneous mode of consciousness is to become more aware of the reality of the situation you're in, and to respond appropriately to that situation. Acting with spontaneity means acting with full responsibility, not with irresponsibility. It means being in a state of consciousness where you're integrating all dimensions of a situation and allowing your deeper analytical and intuitive powers to determine your behavior, rather than operating from external rules and limits.

One of the false assumptions about spontaneous behavior is that it's speedy, erratic, out of control, and unpredictable – but these behaviors come from a very low level of consciousness, the opposite of a truly spontaneous condition. You can be highly spontaneous and be doing absolutely nothing at all. Perhaps your full integration of the situation doesn't lead to action, it leads to quiet reflection. You can certainly be spontaneously meditative and quiet, with calm emotions and zero action.

Likewise, you don't lose control when you're spontaneous – you shift control to a higher mental function that allows you the freedom to do whatever is most appropriate for the situation at hand. Spontaneity implies, in its true meaning, being highly aware of the people you're with and sensitive to their responses and needs – so that you interact with them at optimum levels.

The fear of losing control is, of course, a giant one for all of us. We've been conditioned not to trust our spontaneous impulses. In fact, the very notion of being "impulsive" has a negative connotation. An impulse, though, is nothing more than a flow of information through the nervous system orchestrating a particular action in the body. If the origination of that impulse is from a highly aware, conscious mind, then the action the impulse stimulates will be beautifully controlled by the higher mind.

One thing is sure – you can't be afraid of your own impulses and spontaneous at the same time. This is why I am encouraging you to stop judging yourself and begin trusting who you are. Even if you make a few mistakes along the way, it's important to begin to explore your natural impulses and let them mature so that they fully express your deeper intent and heartfelt emotions.

But, always, yes – you will have to take that leap of spontaneity into letting go of your fear-based worries about doing something wrong and shift into a trust-based quality of consciousness where you honor and respect and trust yourself enough to "set yourself free" in the world.

This step out of worry and into self-trust is the beginning of a truly successful life. And, it's certainly the step you want to lead with as you initiate an encounter at work. You're not going to suddenly "lose control" and do foolish things in the meeting – you're going to shift into a more sincere, spontaneous presence where the other person can truly see who you are and, by experiencing who you really are, learn to trust you. This is the core format of the bonding process that everyone is so eager to make happen.

THE MOMENT OF ENCOUNTER

SETTING YOURSELF FREE

At first you might be thinking that being spontaneous sounds great – but you have no idea how to "get there" into that more expressive honest state of mind. You've been trained by your parents, by your teachers, and certainly by your work experience to control yourself all the time and not to "act impulsively" on the job. Just the opposite, you've done your best to be cautious and present a guaranteed-proper presence at work, so that you won't ever violate any subtle behavior limitations.

> So, even if you want to risk setting yourself free to be more spontaneous in your next business encounter, you have no idea how to actually do that – or do you?

Well, yes, you do. The very first thing you will always want to set free in order to be more genuine and spontaneous in a meeting is simply your own breathing. Your emotions are expressed primarily by your breathing, after all. Every emotion has its particular breath pattern. When you're anxious, your breathing gets tight and shallow (and makes you dizzy and confused). When you're angry, your breathing deepens and charges your body with energy – unless you try to block that anger with muscular tension around the lungs. When you sink into a depressed mood, your breathing becomes flat and loses power. And when you feel good, your breathing deepens, relaxes, and flows effortlessly in and out. Furthermore, when you want to express an emotion, you usually do this through vocalizing on your exhale – as your breathing empowers your voice.

Most people are afraid of their natural emotional expression because of "bad" experiences in the past when they expressed their feelings and got punished for that expression. So, they have the powerful habit of controlling their breathing in an effort to control their emotions. You know that tense feeling in your throat that blocks a sudden outburst when you're angry, or chokes back a sob when you're sad, or constricts your breathing when you're anxious?

Whether you realize it or not, you are usually controlling your breathing – which makes it impossible to be spontaneous.

The first step in relaxing and trusting your own inner feelings is to begin to set free your breathing. And, you do that exactly as I've taught you. There's nothing much more to learn – you simply need to go more deeply into the process. Give this a try even now as you read these words and notice how your breathing begins to relax and feel more free as you focus your attention and say the particular focus phrases.

Turn your mind's focus of attention to the sensation of the air rushing in and out of your nose. To further this shift in focus, you can say to yourself, "I feel the air flowing in and out of my nose." After saying the words, simply observe the sensory happening. Notice if your breathing seems shallow or full, relaxed or tense, at ease and free or tight and controlled.

> Don't try to change anything – instead, allow your direct observation of your breathing to stimulate positive changes in your breathing. That's the first step toward spontaneity – allowing change to happen to your breathing.

And now, let's go to the second step that you already know by expanding your awareness to also include the movements in your chest and belly being caused by your natural breathing process. Say, "I also feel the movements in my chest and belly," and as you experience the breathing sensations in your nose, throat, chest, and belly, be open to a new experience – you've never breathed that breath before. It's new and if you set it free it will be your direct link to your deeper feelings right now.

Let's go another step, one here that will directly encourage positive change in your breath experience. State the direction you want your breath experience to move in: "I am here, now – breathing freely."

TRUSTING EMOTIONAL BALANCE

Homeostasis is one of the most important words in our language, even though most people are just beginning to learn what it means. Its origins are from medicine, but it represents a basic physiological and emotional process of the human organism.

The term *homeostasis* was coined in 1932 by Walter Cannon. It comes from the Greek *homo* (same, like) and *sta* (to stand or stay). Homeostasis is the tendency of the body to seek and maintain a condition of balance or equilibrium within its internal environment even when faced with external changes. A simple example of homeostasis is the body's ability to maintain an internal temperature around 98.6 degrees Fahrenheit regardless of the outside temperature. Homeostasis is the property of an open system that regulates its condition by means of multiple dynamic equilibrium adjustments controlled by interrelated regulation mechanisms. Multicellular organisms require a homeostatic internal environment in order to live; many environmentalists believe this principle also applies to the external environment. Many ecological, biological, and social systems are homeostatic. If the system does not succeed in reestablishing its balance, the system may ultimately stop functioning.

The observation of more and more clinical psychologists and psychiatrists is that the human body also has a natural process for maintaining emotional homeostasis. When a person gets stuck in too much anxiety or stress, very often the body will self-regulate and close down the root cause of the stress or anxiety. As a simple example, when you're caught up in anxiety or blocked emotions and chronically holding your breathing tight, at some point your body will cry out for more oxygen and the yawn or the stretch reflex will activate.

Most of the constriction to your breathing and your free

bodily movement is caused, as we've seen already, by the thoughts and images you chronically allow to dominate your mind. Cognitive psychologists mostly agree that the primary cause of physiological stress is negative, fear-based thought. We can worry ourselves to death, think thoughts that cause terrible tension, and throw our bodies out of balance.

This certainly happens with our breathing. You know how good it feels when your breathing is relaxed and free, deep and expressive of your natural emotions. And, you know how bad it feels when your thoughts and imaginations provoke an anxiety reaction in your body or elicit anger that you then block from expression. And, of course, the shallow flat breathing of depression is a terrible feeling to endure.

But, notice what happens when you simply shine the light of your conscious attention to your breathing, as we just did, and as I hope you are continuing to do as you read these words. As soon as you become conscious that your breathing is being held tense and tight and shallow, the process of homeostasis is activated – and your breathing deepens and feels set free. Ah!

And, as soon as you set your breathing free, your entire system begins to move toward emotional balance and natural functioning. This is the path to becoming emotionally genuine, pure and simple.

I hope you're beginning to understand the depth and complexity of this seemingly simple process. Focus phrases are

THE MOMENT OF ENCOUNTER

activator statements. They initiate a chain reaction inside you. And, all you must do is employ your mind's all-powerful focus of attention precisely where it needs to be held for the body to begin to self-correct and reestablish homeostasis.

As long as you're running on automatic with your attention not focused on your present-moment condition, your body has a very difficult time acting to regain its emotional balance and health. But, as soon as you take your fate in your own conscious hands and choose to aim your attention in such a way as to wake up present-moment awareness of your condition, the self-correcting process cuts into action, and an entire host of alterations is set free to happen.

Over and over I'm telling you to be aware of your breathing at all times. Why am I repeating this rather extreme instruction? Because this breath anchor will serve you so admirably. When you push the breath awareness button, you turn on your entire potential to regain the optimum emotional and physiological condition for the situation you're in. And, in the bargain, you're being nice to yourself. You're quickly shifting from a painful, tense condition in your emotions and muscles to an enjoyable, even downright pleasurable, quality of experience.

"I SET MY BREATHING FREE. I GIVE MYSELF PERMISSION TO FEEL GOOD."

Say it – do it!

SPONTANEOUS RELATING

Let's end this chapter by focusing specifically on the moment of encounter. You've prepared the best you can, using the methods I've taught you and that you'll master over the next few weeks, and now it's time.

At the moment of encounter, most people lose their breath awareness because anxiety grabs them out of habit and reduces their awareness so that the core inner experience is lost. Suddenly you're operating on automatic again with all those old, phony social games and emotional constrictions coming to the fore.

What to do? Slow down, ease up, and allow a little open time and space to come into existence, as we talked about earlier. To do this, shift your attention to the air flowing in and out of your nose . . . and the movements in your chest and belly . . . and then expand to also include the feelings in your heart as you breathe . . . and then expand the full step to be aware of your entire body in the space of the room . . . and expand from that grounded inner center of awareness to also include the person you're meeting.

That's the process. When you lose your inner focus, just move through the process again, even while you're talking. Especially when you're listening to the other person talking, as we'll see in the next section, you will have the opportunity to regain and maintain your inner center.

Bring to mind often the golden words "I give myself permission to feel good." This statement is blunt and short, and gets the job done.

THE MOMENT OF ENCOUNTER

The words will remind your awareness to stay tuned into good feelings in your body regardless of whatever else is happening. Even in difficult social encounters, if you continue to hold the words "I give myself permission to feel good" you'll find that you can be the one in the room that maintains a positive presence – and you'll naturally rise to the top in terms of leadership.

As you set your breathing free, you set your emotions free. You also set your movement free. When you're relaxed and feeling good in your body and aware of your physical presence and posture, the homeostatic function of your nervous system will naturally identify tension postures where you're maintaining stress and you'll spontaneously shift your position and move a little and again help youself feel good. In fact, built into the response of "I give myself permission to feel good" is the permission to move when you want to, to reduce stress, and to generate good feelings in the body.

A basic tenet of feeling good is that the body likes to move. Holding one posture for too long always generates tension and stress. Sometimes, like when practicing yoga, this stillness can evoke particular responses of great value. But, in general, most of the poses we get frozen in are inhibitive postures where we're unconscious of the stress being generated and, therefore, we fail to relieve it.

As soon as you become aware of your entire body at once, here in this present moment, self-correction is empowered and you'll

move so that your body feels less stressed and more at ease. So, give yourself permission to move when you want to – that's being natural and genuine in the other person's presence.

Someone who sits rigid during a conversation is not showing you their genuine feelings at all – they're being inhibited and hiding their feelings, and they're probably caught up in their own version of your general inhibitions. We'll explore in the next section how you can help the other person be more relaxed and spontaneous as part of your service to this person.

For now, let's end this section about the moment of encounter by considering a few more variables of any encounter and exploring how each encounter is going to be in some ways similar to all others, and in some ways unique. The uniqueness of an encounter (this moment has never happened before, you've never felt like you do before, etc.) must always be honored and encouraged. If you're going to succeed with the meeting, it's going to be a unique experience for all involved. It's also why trying to develop a set performance routine of words and behavior to use in every meeting won't really serve you well.

Learning to be spontaneous at meetings is the only sure path to success because, by giving yourself permission to feel free each new moment to respond to the situation naturally, you'll be able to participate in this unique moment fully. You're making sure you're tuned into the uniqueness of the moment so that you can respond to that uniqueness appropriately.

RITUALS ANYONE?

To end this chapter, as we discuss uniqueness of the moment and the value of spontaneous action, I want to mention that certain encounter rituals can also play a valuable role – by helping you create free time and space within which to relate.

All too often, the initial moments of encounter seem hurried, as if there's no free time at all to relate beyond the context of business. But, if you jump right into business, you're not going to have time and space to meet each other heart to heart.

So, I often recommend establishing very minor rituals that you perform when you meet someone. They require time and space to perform – so that you "create" those two necessary ingredients of experience (space and time) during your meeting. For instance, usually you will greet someone while standing and move to where you will conduct your meeting. This movement in itself takes place in time and space, and if you remain highly aware of your body during this movement time, rather than thinking ahead to what you're going to do or say once you get settled, you open up breathing space for both of you.

Let time go by. Don't rush. Enjoy the movements you make. And, when you're settling in, don't instantly begin talking. Allow silence to exist when you can.

By enjoying that moment of silence and peace together, you

THE MOMENT OF ENCOUNTER

can share perhaps the most important interpersonal moment of the meeting – that of simply being together. We are, after all, human beings, which means that our primary identity is not in doing, but in being. Allow time to go by while you simply share space with this person, aware of your breathing, your heart, and your body's presence in the same room as the other person. Take time to experience the other person.

Another way to open up time and space so that the other person can relax into the space is to offer to take a coat or to get a drink – and when you do so, to do this action without any thoughts in your mind at all. The trick of opening up time and space, of course, is the act of quieting the mind and staying tuned acutely and enjoyably into the vastness of the present moment. You are suddenly sharing air with this person, you're being affected by this person's heart and mind, and you're receiving your visual impression of this person. This all takes time – so do what you can to allow time to expand. And, in that time, make yourself a receiver that responds to what you discover – spontaneously.

And, finally, I'm a great fan of settling into a chair across from the person I'm meeting with, or even if standing – and meeting their eyes, and then taking a relaxing breath so that the communication is loud and clear. No pressure here; let's relax and enjoy each other's company. Relax your facial muscles so that you don't have a phony smile in place. Then, allow a slight honest smile to reflect your inward state of peace and openness.

At that point, another ritual that can also happen spontaneously is to begin the conversation not focused on business, but on the personal experience or life of the person you're with. If you need a ritual question, create a set of questions that are genuine. Ask about a recent trip or comment on something positive about the person, or find another way to encourage relaxation and openness.

> And, all the while, remember to also be aware of your own breathing and heart feelings and expand your awareness to take in whatever your senses at all levels are receiving from this person.

If the person seems agitated or upset, you can ask them about how they're feeling so that they can blow off emotional steam. And, if they need to just sit a moment without you pressing them into relating, then, absolutely, relax and give them as much space and time as they need – this can be the greatest gift you give someone who's been pressured for hours before meeting with you. Give them room to relax, give them room to express their inner feelings – give them freedom just like you give yourself freedom!

PROGRAM REVIEW

THE MOMENT OF ENCOUNTER

Quick Review

The moment you meet someone, you need to present an honest, friendly, non-judgmental greeting and offer relaxed breathing space and friendship. Remembering to hold in mind certain focus phrases will help you maintain your bright, inner center, present a genuinely friendly presence, and converse with relaxed spontaneity, acceptance, and enjoyment.

Key Focus Phrases

"I am here now – breathing freely . . ."

"I'm not in any danger . . ."

"I feel grounded in my heart, pelvis, legs, and feet . . ."

"I want to make a new friend . . ."

"I set myself free to feel good right now . . ."

Points to Remember

Please memorize and hold in mind the following four steps as you enter into an encounter. Prepare yourself for a positive encounter with whomever you're meeting –

purposefully choose the quality of consciousness that makes genuine relating possible. You can just say these four short statements to yourself, even while you're beginning your encounter. The words will linger in the back of your mind and strongly influence your mood and presence.

1. Stop hurting: By turning your attention to your breathing experience, you will quickly snap out of your mental push and into the future, and retain the organic sense of your body's own pace, breath by breath, through the unfolding present moment.

2. Start feeling: By also being aware of the feelings in your heart as you breathe, you will shift from thought to emotion – and further expand your awareness of the world in the here and now. Be heart centered and your client will be able to respond accordingly.

3. Create free time: By expanding your awareness in the present moment to include good feelings in your body, and also by tuning into the sounds and sights and scents around you, you enter into an awareness of open space where you can enjoyably share space with others.

THE MOMENT OF ENCOUNTER

4. Relax and expand: By insisting on the freedom to enjoy the present moment and to honor your own right to feel good, you relax and tap into genuine positive feelings in your heart and expand your awareness bubble to include the person you're with in a friendly way.

Reflection Time

Again, I recommend that you find time to sit quietly for at least a few minutes to see what the following questions provoke deep inside you. Please move through this same process at least three or four times in the next weeks and months so that you tap unexpected inner wisdom and truth. First, tune into your breathing and your heart . . . then read the question . . . then return your awareness to your breathing and your heart . . . then read the question again . . . close your eyes, and see what insights might spring to mind, new each time.

A. In a business encounter, can you put aside your judgments and accept the person you're meeting with just as they are? What might happen if you do this in all of your relationships?

B. Is your mind's awareness a variable that you can

learn to expand? How do you feel about including other people in your awareness bubble and "sharing space" with someone consciously?

C. Are you usually well grounded in your physical body or are you usually fixated in your thoughts, memories, and plans? Do you see a business or sales value in learning to become more grounded in your body?

D. Do you believe that your mind and heart have the power to influence the thoughts and feelings of another person? If so, how does this impact your business life?

E. Trust and respect are big words – how do you feel about offering trust and respect to business associates?

Exercise: Staying Grounded

That first moment of encounter happens so fast – and is so important. Here's what's most important to hold in mind, and to do, at that moment.

1. Prepare: Preparation is certainly half the story of successfully encountering someone. Be sure to move

through either the one- or two-minute process you learned earlier – and also do your regular homework for enhancing your power to come from the heart and make genuine contact. Say to yourself, "I am here now – breathing freely."

2. Get grounded: Right when you come face to face with someone, train yourself to hold your primary attention to your breathing – to the air flowing in and out, the movements in your chest and belly, and to your ongoing feeling of being grounded. Say to yourself, "I feel grounded in my heart, pelvis, legs, and feet."

3. Share space: Expand your awareness to include the air around you – the space you're now sharing with this person. Let this shared medium bond the two of you and hold your attention in the present moment. Say to yourself, "I want to make a new friend."

4. Be spontaneous: Rather than acting from a planned script, just relax, give yourself permission to enjoy yourself, and let your body move spontaneously. Say to yourself, "I set myself free to feel good right now."

Practice mastering this process – give yourself time to play with this inner method and don't be upset when you slip back into old habits. Just keep returning to the process, moving through it again and again.

AUDIO SCRIPT: CLASS TWO

Go to www.listeningwithempathy.com for audio guidance.

At the moment of encounter, you want to make sure that you don't contract emotionally and go temporarily unconscious – instead, you will want to take certain inner steps to guarantee that you remain bright and centered in the present moment, and available for immediate heart contact.

Imagine that you're approaching someone, or they're coming toward you. Stay aware of the air flowing in and out of your nose, and hold in your mind the focus phrase "I'm not in any danger here." If you feel detached from your body, say to yourself, "I feel grounded in my heart, pelvis, legs, and feet" and allow those words to drop your attention down into your power center.

Rather than becoming tense and acting out of habit, give yourself permission to act spontaneously, and say to yourself, "I set myself free to feel good right now." And, to state your clear intent, say either "I want to make a new friend" or "I am here to serve, flourish, and enjoy life."

After a few weeks of practice with this audio class, you'll find that these focus phrases will become the supporting background that holds your focus in optimum directions during the moment of encounter. As you meet someone with an open heart and a confident, friendly attitude, your business with them will unfold within the atmosphere of trust, mutual respect, and shared success!

Empathic Communication

CHAPTER 7

LISTEN WITH CALM COMPASSION

We now approach the heart of any business meeting, after you've paused to spend a bit of social time together – and are ready to talk business. Everything we've talked about thus far has been preparation for this main event. Now is the time to focus clearly on your higher business intent to identify the customer's need and to do your best to satisfy that need, while also doing your best to make a sale or provide a service that is beneficial to your employer and yourself.

This is the crucial point where too many people suddenly stop listening with empathy and lock into manipulative attitudes and behavior that violate the bonding process. What can you do to successfully navigate phase three and stay in heart contact with your customer throughout the meeting?

Here are the key points to hold in mind:

- Listen, listen, listen: In order to ensure that your customer feels acknowledged and well served, make sure you consciously focus on being a sincere listener. The person you're meeting with has a driving need of some sort to satisfy – and your first action, therefore, needs to be to let this person talk to you and explain that need. In this chapter, we will explore more of the subtle nuances of successful listening.

- Put service first: As you are quiet and listen to your client's expression of their needs, and as you begin thinking about how you can best act to meet their needs, be sure that you hold in mind that your primary intent is not to pressure the person into a sale, but to make sure that the person is truly served by your actions. This is the only way to make sure of customer loyalty – be loyal to them first. We'll talk this all through in the next chapter.

- Engage beyond the product: And, finally, be sure that as the meeting comes to an end you engage again with the customer "beyond the product," which means that you focus on them as a person you've just met and whom you want to see again. Allow your heart to stay open and your warmth to continue with genuine expression so that the person feels appreciated not just from a commerce point of view, but also from the point of view of a valued friend. The final chapter of this third section will explore this theme.

EMPATHIC COMMUNICATION

LISTENING WITH HEART

Let's get down to absolute basics. First of all, listening requires a particular focus of your attention toward the auditory function of your nervous system. Vibrational information comes into your mind, and you process this information into meaningful words and concepts – and then reflect upon that auditory input. The amount of your attention that you focus on what you're actually hearing determines if you're a good listener or a distracted one.

In my work as a psychologist, I've observed that most of us don't seem to listen very well at all. We tend to focus more of our attention on what we're going to say back to a person than on the words that person is actually speaking. We don't give people our full listening attention by any means – because our attention is one step in the future, imagining our clever reply.

When you are with a client or co-worker, you have a gift to give them that they will instantly appreciate and respond to – your full listening attention. But, what if your listening habits are strongly attached to a tendency to focus more on your own thoughts than on the thoughts of the other person – how do you break out of this chronic and quite universal "what did you say" habit?

Again, the solution begins at the same point – your awareness of your breathing in the present moment. Your thoughts pull you out of the present moment – so do something that brings you back to where the person's voice is happening.

> Just remember to hold half of your attention on your own breathing experience and present-moment physical presence in the room. Hold the other half of your attention on the words that the person is speaking and on taking in the person's visual presence as well.

What happens when you hold your focus of attention on two or more sensory events at the same time? All thoughts stop. That's your instant solution to not being a good listener. Just say to yourself the focus phrase shorthand: "breath . . . heart . . . voice," and experience your own breathing – plus also the feelings in your heart, plus also the words that the other person is speaking. There! You're entirely present for that person!

You'll need to exercise this cognitive-shifting function over and over during the next weeks to master this "full attention" listening. Give yourself time – but remember that if you don't practice this process, you won't get good at it. I've made the process just as simple as possible because I know how difficult it is to perform a complex inner process right in the middle of a meeting. But, there's nothing stopping you from memorizing three words and repeating them to yourself while you're listening to someone talking to you. "Breath . . . heart . . . voice."

At first you'll find that your attention jumps back and forth from your breathing to your heart to the person's voice you're listening to. But, suddenly you'll experience an expansion of your awareness to where you can do all three simultaneously, as an

EMPATHIC COMMUNICATION

integrated "listening from the heart" experience. This is your aim – to be present for this person, fully hearing what they're saying and without having half your attention busy thinking about what to say next. That's listening with heart – and the person will notice that you're "present for them" and deeply appreciate it.

WHAT ABOUT STRATEGY?

I'm well aware that a lot of you have been trained with special sales strategies that you want to employ in a business meeting – and you're concerned that if you quiet your thoughts entirely that you'll forget your sales attack and lose the momentum of the sale. I assure you that just the opposite will usually happen. And, hold this in mind: If you don't really listen with heart to the needs of the customer, if you're caught up in past strategies and future projections, you're not going to be "in touch" with the customer's needs because you will fail to listen clearly to them. And, without knowing the customer's needs, how can you satisfy them?

Without first listening with sincerity, your pre-programmed sales rap will fall on deaf ears – because what you're saying in response to what the customer just said to you isn't actually a response to their need. It's just your canned sales spiel.

The best strategy in sales, from my understanding in our current customer-first marketplace, is the strategy of fully understanding the needs of the customer, and then responding

spontaneously with the best solution your expanded reasoning and creativity comes up with. The sales person with the most incoming data of customer needs will always outdo the sales person who failed to pay full attention to customer data. So, logic dictates letting go of clever pre-game strategies in favor of responses to customer needs that are genuine and in full resonance with what the customer just communicated to you.

And, again, we come to the psychological dynamics of spontaneity, this time in relation to the mind's creative functioning. A customer or client has a particular need – or they wouldn't be spending time with you in the first place. In most cases, fulfilling their need can be somewhat complex. If you fully listen to what they say to you, and then shift into creative problem-solving mode after they've had their say, you can activate your full creative spark and instantly flash with a great idea to offer the client.

It's the same in corporate meetings – listen first to comprehend the dilemma as fully as you can with an open, focused, receptive mind. And then, shift into present-moment, spontaneous, creative mode to see what great ideas might come to you. "Clear, devoted listening in – sharp, realistic ideas out."

CUSTOMER EXPERIENCE AGAIN

Meanwhile, what is the client or customer or co-worker experiencing while you listen with your full attention and here-and-now presence? The customer is experiencing something that is quite rare and that feels absolutely wonderful – someone really listening

EMPATHIC COMMUNICATION

to them! Even if the first thing the customer does is blow off steam by talking about some unrelated incident in the street outside, if you take time to truly listen to that person, they will love you for it – and, as a result, you will earn yourself a loyal customer.

> Behind all this is solid psychological fact – people need to be heard in order to heal. You know what a relief it is to be able to relate a stressful experience to a friend.

Therapy is based on the fact that something special happens to us when we tell someone something important to us, and actually have that other person take in what we say. This is what makes a good friend truly invaluable – they listen to us without judgment and often without saying anything. They just take in what we say so that we have shared our experience. And, in the sharing of the experience, something happens inside us. We get "it" off our chests and out into the open, and we are relieved of carrying "it" all alone.

So, regardless of the first thing that someone begins a meeting talking about, be a good listener. They have a first need, obviously, to unburden themselves or to express something wonderful they just saw or to tell you their hope and plans. Whatever it is, let it come out. Be a friend, even if this is your first meeting. This is the core of customer bonding. Be there for the other person, if only for a few moments. Put aside your driving intent long enough to really hear what they have to say. Then you can have your chance for doing what you want to do with them.

OBNOXIOUS CLIENTS

Early in this book we mentioned the ongoing challenge of dealing with the negative moods of bothersome customers. Perhaps right now you're thinking that everything I'm saying is doable as long as the customer is a nice person. But, what about when you have to deal with someone you immediately don't like, who's in a foul mood, who has a nasty personality, or who has a bothersome intent? Can you still be friendly, stay open, and have a positive experience with such a person?

Well, there are some cases in which you probably can't. There are rotten apples out there, and you're going to encounter your share. However, I still insist that the same principles apply and that you can employ the same approach with the sour apples that you do with the peaches and cream. And, here's the logic.

When you come together with another person who is caught up in a more contracted, unfriendly, negative emotional mood than you are, one of three things is going to happen. Either you're going to be strong and positive and help bring this person's mood up, this person's negative mood is going to drag you down – or you're going to back off from each other and not influence each other's moods.

I challenge you always to see if you can stay positive and help brighten the other person's mood a bit. In the long run, they'll love you for it and become a dedicated customer – specifically because you were kind to them when they were feeling so terrible. Their primary need was emotional help, and you provided it.

EMPATHIC COMMUNICATION

How do you stay bright when someone comes at you with negative attitudes and emotions? I hate to sound like a music loop, but my same basic principle applies here, and even more urgently. When someone pops your expanded emotional bubble and brings you down into their negative mood, you lose your awareness of your own breathing and drop out of your enjoyment of the present moment. So I say – don't let anyone do that to you!

If you realize that you're suddenly sharing space and time with someone who threatens your inner peace and pleasure in the here and now, pull back inwardly so that you continue to stay aware of the air flowing in and out of your nose or mouth and the movements in your chest and belly – hold onto your breath anchor for all you're worth. That's your lifeline to good feelings and positive action. Don't let go of it.

> Even if you have to temporarily lose most of your awareness of the world around you, hold onto your inner calm and brightness. And then, to whatever extent you can, expand to also include this person in your positive bubble.

Find that inner balance where you can stay okay inside your own skin, while also taking in a bit of the other person's presence. Don't do this in a judgmental way – that will make the situation worse. Don't flaunt your good feelings. Just insist on your right to stay positive in the present moment regardless of what the world throws at you. There's your strength. Develop that strength by exercising it regularly.

When I find myself with someone who's quite a bother to be around, I often physically step back one or two paces, or just lean back an inch in my chair so that I feel I have breathing room of my own. Then I say silently to this person as a special focus phrase, "I'm happy to help you feel better if you want." Inside your own psyche, make this friendly offer, not as a judgment, just as a nice thing to offer to someone who's obviously hurting inside.

You'll be surprised at the percentage of times that the other person will, step by step, recover from their bummer mood and brighten in response to your unspoken offer of acceptance and brightness. Perhaps you'll still have to sit there and listen to a few minutes of complaining or judgment from them. You don't have to think about what they're saying or react to it; you just give them space to speak their mind without you reacting.

This certainly applies to upset colleagues, spouses, children, and all the rest. Be someone who will listen to people when they're upset. Be there for them. That's what empathy is – feeling another person's pain as well as their pleasure. You don't have to be polluted by their outbursts. You simply have to accept them as they are right then.

You never know what might have just happened to someone before they meet with you. That's the part of the equation that you don't know. But, for whatever reason, if they're upset or angry or depressed, they probably need to talk about what has them upset before they can get down to business. So, go ahead. Let them blow. Create a bit of neutral time and space

EMPATHIC COMMUNICATION

where they can unburden themselves. If, perchance, your boss complains that you're playing therapist rather than closing a deal, then perhaps your boss needs to take a bit of time to understand this deeper dimension of sales – because the logic rings true.

SPEAKING YOUR MIND

Of course, at some point you will need to draw limits. I'm not suggesting that you forget your sales or service role and just go around listening to people all the time. You also have your right to speak your mind and discuss your side of the bargain. Some people don't know when to stop talking. And some people will sap your emotional strength with non-stop complaining.

If you make your offer of being a good listener, and then realize that the other person is going too long and violating your own rights to be listened to and heard, then by all means, exercise your right to break in and shift the focus of the meeting in the direction the situation implies.

Always be the first to offer to listen. If the person you're meeting with is not ready to express their needs, you will need to start the conversation, perhaps by sharing your personal feelings so that you allow the other person to be a good listener. Friendship implies a two-way listening/talking relationship. But, hold in mind that you want to open up space and time for the other person to share their needs. This is the wise and compassionate act of both a friend and a successful sales/service person.

You've been listening to me for quite some time. Let me do something I often do in my books: actually create time and space for a break in the flow of words so that you can put the book aside, quiet the flow of ideas and suggestions – and tune into your own reflections about everything you've read.

What do you have to say about becoming a master listener? What are your memories and ideas about how to make customers enjoy your company? Do you agree with my line of logic here, or do you have a different understanding of all this?

When you pause right now, put the book aside for a few moments or longer and experience your breathing and your heart. What thoughts come spontaneously to mind?

PAUSE & EXPERIENCE

CHAPTER 8

SERVE WITH GENUINE INTENT

One of the curious paradoxes of business is that two people can do the exact same type of job at work, and yet operate with opposite intents. Whereas one person may see their work as honest service, the other person can see the same work as purely selfish in which their own needs are what are important, not their client's.

In this chapter I want to explore in depth with you the constant choices you are making regarding your core attitudes toward the work you do. By unearthing this underlying substratum of your work stance, you can evaluate if this stance truly serves you or if you might do better to choose a new one.

Specifically, does a person succeed optimally through being self-centered and selfishly grabbing all they can, or does success actually emerge more predictably if we let go of a fear-based, selfish stance at work (there's not enough to go around so I'm going to grab all I can) and shift into an empathy-based stance where the aim is truly to be of service to others?

Take the example of George in his insurance sales role. Before he began training in this method, he operated out of an inherited attitude that assumed there was not enough to go around and that if he didn't put himself first and grab all he could, he might have to do without. His underlying motivation in life was grounded in the beliefs of his father and grandparents, of scarcity being the rule of life. Assuming that there wasn't enough for all, as a child he'd feared actually not having any food to eat.

He saw his father grabbing all he could and using manipulative sales techniques to amass considerable excess of wealth so that the fear of scarcity was pushed farther and farther away. But, because the entire mindset of his family was based on selfish grabbing rather than on participating in a service-centered economy, as an adult he simply continued with the selfish, fearful emotions and attitudes and behavior that had driven his parents.

Of course, there have been and probably will be hard times for at least some members of our society and certainly our world. My point isn't that we don't live with the danger of scarcity. My point is that, realistically, being driven by fears of not having enough and basing your stance at work on that fear-based belief will directly undermine your ability to actually succeed and avoid scarcity in your life. Again, the logic is tight and worth looking at.

EMPATHIC COMMUNICATION

COMPETITION OR COOPERATION

Capitalism is based on an open, competitive market where some companies rise to the top and succeed while others fail and fall away. There is a constant shifting and changing in the marketplace. But at the level of employment, except in periods of temporary economic crash, most people in most societies can find work. There are clearly exceptions in the world that need to be addressed, but in these exceptions the culprit isn't cooperation and service-oriented attitudes at work, but rather greed and fear-based, selfish attitudes.

Competition drives companies to do their best and to produce good products and services at the lowest costs possible. This is a plus in the world economy. At the macro level, it does seem that companies competing against each other in the marketplace works better than the state trying to manipulate the marketplace.

At the micro level inside each company, however, competition among employees tends to deter progress and success, whereas a solid cooperative team spirit tends to advance progress and success.

This is true because companies are living organisms for which the individuals within it are all working together for a greater cause and purpose – the success of the company. When individual cells in the organism begin fighting rather than cooperating with each other, a definite condition of ill-

ness and collapse begins to develop. Except in very particular and isolated instances, competition within a company has proven much less effective than cooperation.

So, you might want to take a look at your own attitudes and see if you're arriving at work with an ingrained one-liner motivating you to fight to dominate your fellow workers, or if you arrive at work with the intent to participate fairly and serve your company and your co-workers the best you can. What attitudes did you inherit from your family and society and what attitudes do you think will serve you best in the future?

You do have the power to see this larger situation clearly, and to decide which stance to take at work. Much of this book and my online training programs are aimed to advance your intent in these directions.

EVERYONE SERVING EVERYONE

I remember a truly brilliant anthropology professor at Princeton who one morning explained to our class his greater economic vision that everyone in the world served everyone else in the world, all the time. His vision was that we live in a mutually serving society where each action we make at work is, upon close examination, an act of service to others – even if we perceive it as a greedy act to help serve no one but ourselves.

Perhaps you've thought this through yourself already, but let's make sure we're all on the same page here. The whole point

EMPATHIC COMMUNICATION

of a business or money-based system of any kind is that you identify a human need and, in exchange for money, help satisfy that need. If there's no need, then no one is going to pay you for doing something. But if there is a need, then in exchange for money, you serve that person by helping to satisfy the need.

> There is really no other realistic way to see anyone's job at work except as a service being performed for money or exchange. We're all serving other people – that's what work is.

Even the highest-up executive roles are purely service roles. The CEO is there to serve the board, and to serve the employees by guiding them to success in their work. The investors are serving the company by providing the needed capital. The managers are serving the employees, executives, and shareholders by making sure work gets done properly and on time. So, it's not just the janitors who are in servant roles in a company or society – everyone gets up each day and goes to work specifically to serve the needs of others. Otherwise, there's no business and no paycheck.

Historically, there has always been a negative connotation to the term "servant" because of the traditional relationship between an indentured servant or slave and that person's master. And, definitely, those relationships were often entirely unfair. But, by making the role relationships fairer we didn't do away with the notion of being of service to others in order to survive and thrive ourselves.

So, I encourage you to look at your attitudes about being a servant and being of service to others. How do you feel about serving others? Does it make you feel good to be of service or do you fight against the very idea of playing the servant role? Furthermore, do you agree with me that we're all serving each other or are you somehow outside that mutual-service interaction?

PAUSE & EXPERIENCE

SERVING YOUR CUSTOMER

Let's get more specific now. George at first found the whole idea of serving others unappealing. He liked the feeling that he really worked for himself and didn't have to serve anybody. His mother had once had to clean other people's houses and do their laundry when money was tight in his family. She resented the servant role and his father hated seeing her as a servant for rich people. So, George carried around a negative stance toward the entire idea of being of service to others. In fact, he liked having other people serve him because it made him feel powerful and on top of others.

George also felt isolated and lonely and somehow cut off from the people around him. He was a highly judgmental person who tended to put "down" everyone around him to boost his own ego. When he'd meet with an insurance client, his inner thoughts were often of contempt and derision – he disliked people who let him manipulate them even though he was making money off them. And, instead of feeling that he was serving his clients, he carried the attitude that he was making loads of money by cleverly manipulating them.

We've seen the final results of the greed-based selfish attitudes that George carried around and projected on the world. Rather than genuinely making heart contact and sharing in a sense of cooperation with his clients, he alienated them.

> Rather than feeling good in his heart that he was able to meet his clients' needs with his insurance package, George laughed all the way to the bank with each sale – and ended up alone, made fewer sales, and felt terrible in his heart.

Furthermore, his health declined because rather than feeling relaxed and fulfilled and part of a larger community, he felt all alone and, therefore, vulnerable and insecure.

People like George often take a bit of time to begin to grasp the fact that their negative attitudes could be sabotaging their lives – but when they see the logic, they do usually "get it" and seek change in their lives. As we have seen, our attitudes and emotions do have a powerful tendency to seek homeostasis and a healthy inner balance. And as soon as we begin to realize that our old negative attitudes aren't serving us at all, we initiate a natural shift in one-liners away from self-destructive, fear-based attitudes toward more successful, positive attitudes.

HELPFUL SERVICE HINTS

It's very easy to slip into old attitudes and behavioral patterns with clients that disrupt the positive mood of friendly service. Here are a few pointers to hold in mind and to prime yourself with before a business encounter. After a meeting, be sure to review this list and evaluate how well you did and what you might do differently next time.

- Service Hint One: Remember to stay aware of your breathing and your heart so that you're serving the client by offering your full attention.

- Service Hint Two: Make sure that you take time to truly listen to the needs of the person you're with so that they feel you're interested in them and there to help where you can in realistic ways.

- Service Hint Three: Hold in your mind the focus phrase, "I'm here to help this person with their needs." Say this to yourself as a basic statement of intent several times during the meeting.

- Service Hint Four: Rather than feeling that you must make an effort to push your business intent onto your client, focus on the desire to identify their need and to do something if you can to fulfill that need.

- Service Hint Five: If you can't optimally fulfill their need, or if someone or some different product can, serve your customer by advising them of this.

EMPATHIC COMMUNICATION

SELF-SACRIFICE MAKES SENSE

The fifth hint I just offered might at first seem like bad business advice. How can it be of any benefit to your company if you tell a customer to go down the street to your competitor who has a product or service that will better meet the needs of the customer?

A successful company is an organism that wants to live a long and prosperous life, not just grab all it can in the short term and then wither away. This is why short-term, selfish acts on the part of an employee will almost always damage that company in the long run.

> In general, thinking in the short term without considering long-term effects has proven a seriously damaging strategy in business, even though at times the pressure of short-term profits does drive a corporation into greedy postures and actions.

In the long run, as I'm sure you know, customers who realize you sold them an inferior product or failed to help them get the best service will not return to do more business with you. Furthermore, they'll complain to their friends and your reputation will become tarnished. And these twin poles of loyal customers and bright reputation are what ensure success in a company.

Many employees still struggle with managers and owners who fail to realize that temporary sacrifice often leads to long-term profits. If you have someone "over" you who complains when you serve a customer by not making a sale, perhaps you can explain this logic to them until it becomes company policy to put service ahead of short-term profits.

This basic logic also applies to everything else you might do in life. The person who puts service first in community, family, and business ends up receiving more than the person who is stingy and only helps when there's an immediate, personal payback. With money as well as energy and love, the old adage "what goes around comes around" has proven true the world over. Give love and you'll receive love. Give of your attention and your energy and people will respond by offering you attention and energy. But be stingy and you'll find that the flow dries up.

> So, if you want to receive, don't worry about receiving – give freely and be of service to others and your life will be bountiful.

Furthermore, it just happens to feel good to give. Your heart sings when you're being of service to others. Your stress goes down and your health blossoms when you're involved in cooperative group activities. And, as you help other people in your community to do better, you strengthen the community that also sustains you.

When we focus on greed and selfish actions, we cut off the vitality that nurtures life. When we focus on giving and sharing, we increase that vitality. And, when we enter into each new business meeting with the intent to enjoy the experience of being of compassionate service, we boost sales as well as good feelings. Clear logic. Put it into action!

EMPATHIC COMMUNICATION

C H A P T E R   9

ENGAGE BEYOND THE PRODUCT

We've now considered what you can do to boost your empathy quotient before an encounter, right at the beginning of an encounter, and in the middle of the encounter. In this chapter, we're going to look at the best way to end an encounter. Perhaps you've made a sale, closed a contract, or performed your service successfully for this person or group. Perhaps you have not completed a sale or contract or whatever other intent you had in the business meeting. Regardless of the business outcome, I recommend that you end the meeting with the following hints firmly in mind.

First of all, do the same thing that you did to initiate the encounter. Take a deep breath and create breathing space for the other person so that you don't just suddenly pull your attention away from them and desert them.

Remember that your last moments together may quite possibly

stand as the primary impression the customer takes with them and remembers. So, be sure to stay conscious and focused on the person, and to allow a bit of time and space to come into being for an enjoyable parting experience.

Perhaps the best way to ensure a positive parting is to again say to yourself, "I give myself permission to feel good right now" and to let those words focus your attention on your own inner experience. Hold in mind that as soon as you turn your attention to your tensions, they will immediately begin to ease up. Perhaps you stand up and walk toward each other as part of your process for saying goodbye, which provides a perfect opportunity to enjoy the movement and to return more fully to your whole-body awareness in the present moment. And, obviously, regaining full awareness of your breathing and your heart will serve you as well for ending an encounter as for beginning one.

Also, no matter what has happened during the meeting, be sure to end it by letting go of commerce entirely and, with an accepting mind and mood, enjoy this person's company as you part. Let your heart be open to accept the person just as they are – and enjoy your own presence equally. With your heart warm and open and receptive to experiencing this person's presence, just "be" with this person for a moment.

That's how bonding takes place – enjoying the simple experience of sharing time and space with each other. That's what friendship is all about.

EMPATHIC COMMUNICATION

Beyond the Game

The two of you (or perhaps more) have been playing a mutu-ally accepted game together during your meeting. You have come together for a possible positive exchange of service, help, goods, and money. You've been playing the company rep role, the other person's been playing the customer role. This is all well and good because commerce is a definite part of our lives.

However, to begin and end a meeting you will benefit greatly from popping out of your let's-do-commerce role and once again, as you did in the beginning of the meeting, relate with the person beyond the confines, strictures, and definitions of your business/consumer roles. Throughout this book I've been encouraging you to take time to learn how to just be yourself. At the end of a meeting is a prime time to know how to rapidly let go of your role and just "be with" the other person.

Again – how can you best do this? Establish the powerful habit of remembering to drop down to your breath anchor. Tune into your heart feelings. Expand your awareness of the sensory events happening in the here and now. Get out of your head and your plans and your mental games and wake up to you as the other person is seeing you – as a body in space and time, moving and expressing your basic personality and emotions and intent.

For an instant, shift into your body, be aware of two parts of your body at once – your feet and your head at once, for instance. And expand from that polarity to include the volume of your body. And expand again to tune into all the sounds around you and your sense of the volume of the room.

Go totally three-dimensional and heart-focused so that you're fully present in your body for your goodbye. Let the person feel the impact of your presence as a human being, not just you as a sales person.

FORGET THE PRODUCT

As long as your customer feels that you're trying to get something from them there exists a distance and even a tension between the two of you. Hopefully you've minimized this tension through my suggestions in earlier chapters. And now, as you prepare to end the encounter, you can let that tension drop entirely.

See the person beyond your fixation on their need and your need. Let go of the survival game and let go of your identity as representing the company and its product or service.

Who are you when you're not in sales and service mode? Hopefully you're someone who knows how to "be" in the present moment, living spontaneously in response to what's happening around you. When you temporarily let go of all your thoughts about intentions and needs, you can relax and just do nothing unless you feel spontaneously moved to participate in what's naturally happening around you.

This means that if you're in a room with someone who's getting set to leave and go on with their day, this person is what's happening around you, and so you respond to this person, and

EMPATHIC COMMUNICATION

"dance the same goodbye dance" that they're dancing. As you stay aware of your breathing and your heart and your whole-body presence, you respond to their movements, perhaps shake hands or walk with them to the door. And, you enjoy the movement and their presence and the basic feeling of sharing space and time with them.

The words that you say can certainly be spontaneous; however, do hold one intent still in your mind – that of encouraging this person to come back again. Often the moment of parting in a business meeting is the phoniest of the whole time spent together – especially on the part of the employee who wants to somehow manipulate the customer into returning. So, be especially careful here.

Rather than feeling anxious that the person might not return and acting overly friendly and saying insincere words, do your best to stay calm and focus inward on your heart. Find a radiance of warmth and acceptance to project out to the other person, and touch them with a bit of compassion.

> This parting act of friendship can be quite subtle. But, the primary rule always holds – you've got to feel it, to express it. So only act if you spontaneously feel moved.

Wait for that inner spark – otherwise don't do much of anything because you'll come across as fake. Give yourself a few weeks to master this positive parting act. Hold onto your genuine feelings as well as you can, even if they're not especially strong at first. You'll soon discover that it feels good to relax and not to push at the end of a meeting – but rather to allow a natural flow of feelings and movement to end the encounter in a unique, spontaneous way.

WORDS THAT HELP

Having said all that, I'm now going to also recommend another dimension to the parting experience – using certain focus phrases that express your intent honestly and openly, and without manipulation. Almost certainly you have a habitual repertoire of parting phrases that you use at the end of a meeting. These are probably just fine to continue using – as long as the feeling behind them is conscious and genuine.

You do have intent as the person leaves. The intent is to see this person return to your company at some point in the future because you need to make a living through customer loyalty.

So, if you're naturally and honestly feeling this intent and need, you can state the desire openly so that you leave the customer with this final expression of your own need and hope regarding them.

The trick is in having these words emerge from your heart. There's no room for preprogrammed mental concepts. For instance, you might say on parting, "Hope to see you again!" If you're saying this to pressure the person to return, then don't say it at all. But if you're feeling a heart contact with this

EMPATHIC COMMUNICATION

person and really do hope to see them again because you've felt a friendship bond forming with them, then saying these words is not only honest, but also important to both of you.

You might also end the meeting, if you sold a product, by saying, "I hope that works just right for you!" And if said from the heart, you can truly mean this statement as well. Or, you might say, "I hope you enjoyed my service (whatever it is)" and, "Come again soon!" With your heart behind the words, you'll impact the customer so that they feel well liked and welcome to return. You'll also be placing a "welcome tag" in their minds that they'll remember – because they'll associate your words with your warm emotion. This association will strongly encourage them to return.

PROGRAM REVIEW

DOING BUSINESS WITH HEART

Quick Review

When you begin talking business, you need to maintain your clear intent to genuinely be of service and to enable your customer to truly satisfy their needs. By encouraging an enjoyable emotional atmosphere you can make sure the customer feels in good hands and well taken care of. And, by staying in friendly "service" mode, you guarantee that your customer or client will want to return and do business with you again.

Key Focus Phrases
"I want to listen to this person's needs . . ."
"I choose to help this person satisfy their needs . . ."
"I want us both to win today . . ."
"I'm here to enjoy this experience . . ."

Points to Remember
It's all too easy to slip into old behavioral patterns with clients that disrupt the positive mood of friendly service. Here are key pointers to hold in mind and to prime yourself with before a business encounter. After a meeting, be sure to review this list and to evaluate how well you did in this "service" dimension and what you might do differently next time:

- Service Hint One: Remember to stay aware of your breathing and your heart so that you're serving the client by offering your full attention.

- Service Hint Two: Make sure that you take time to truly listen to the needs of the person you're with so that they feel you're interested in them and there to help where you can in realistic ways.

- Service Hint Three: Hold in your mind the focus phrase, "I'm here to help this person with their needs." Say this to yourself as a basic statement of intent several times during the meeting.

- Service Hint Four: Rather than feeling that you must make an effort to push your business intent onto your client, focus on your desire to identify their need and to do something if you can to fulfill that need.

- Service Hint Five: If you can't optimally fulfill their need, or if someone or some different product can, truly serve your customer by advising them of this.

EMPATHIC COMMUNICATION

Reflection Time

Throughout this discussion, we've been exploring the basic dynamic of what happens when you silence the habitual flow of thoughts through your mind and become quiet in your mind or say certain focus phrases to shift your attention in desired inner directions. Here's a set of questions related to this process:

1. Psychological judo: What happens in your mind when you refocus your attention to two or more physical sensations at the same time – the air flowing in and out of your nose (sensation #1) and the movements in your chest and belly as you breathe (sensation #2)?

2. Relating without judgment: Fixating on judgmental thoughts blocks heartfelt emotions from being felt and expressed. Saying the phrase "I honor and respect the person I'm working with" aims your attention toward doing just that. How do you respond when you say these words to yourself?

3. Loving yourself first: You can't feel warm and empathic toward another person when you're feeling the opposite toward yourself. When you say to yourself, "I feel good toward my own self,"

what thoughts and emotions arise? Are you ready to love yourself unconditionally?

4. Being spontaneous: When you're lost in thought, you're gone from the present moment – and if you're not focused on the present moment, you can't engage with other people heart to heart or be spontaneous in your expressions and actions. How do you feel about becoming more spontaneous at work?

5. Enjoying being of service: You have the choice of perceiving your work as greedy manipulation of others in order to satisfy your needs or as friendly, empathic service in order to satisfy your customer's needs. When you say to yourself, "I'm here to be of service," what feelings are evoked? Do you really want to help other people in life?

6. Listening with compassion: You cannot satisfy a customer's needs until you listen to their expression of their needs. Listening with a quiet mind and a receptive heart is the core of empathic bonding. But, can you do this? What happens when you listen with your full attention?

7. Creating time and space to relate: All relating

takes place within time and space. If you don't feel you have time for anything but business with a client, then you won't be able to experience heart contact with this person. Are you able to slow down, take a deep breath, and just "be" with someone? And what happens when you do?

8. Making every moment a choice: Each new moment you spend with a customer, co-worker, or client is an opportunity to remain open and conscious and friendly – or to sink into habitual mental and emotional moods where you lose heart contact. What are your habits – and how do you feel about choosing to spend time in the coming weeks and months mastering these simple yet essential mood-management methods?

Exercise: Business with Heart

You want to make money when you're at work. You want to serve and sell and succeed. The question is how best to do that – and at the same time respect and honor both yourself and your client. You have learned in the first two sections of this book how to prepare for a positive interaction and stay heart centered during the moment of encounter. Now you're set to do business while remaining empathic and in service mode.

EMPATHIC COMMUNICATION

1. The secret lies in memorizing and holding in mind several focus phrases that enable you to remain aware of the underlying qualities of heart and mind that keep you positive and compassionate while doing business. Primary among these focus phrases is "I want to listen to this person's needs."

2. After you have listened well and heard the person's needs, it's time to shift into being of service and seeing if you can satisfy those needs. Say to yourself, "I want to help this person satisfy their needs." Hold this clear intent in the back of your mind while you're listening and talking to your customer. You'll feel good with this intent in your heart – and by feeling good and helpful, you'll encourage a win-win interaction with your client.

3. And, throughout, rather than getting tight and tense when advancing your business intent, also hold the focus phrase "I'm here to enjoy this experience" in mind. Customers will then relax and enjoy your presence – and want to return to do business with you again!

AUDIO SCRIPT: CLASS THREE

Go to www.listeningwithempathy.com for audio guidance.

In this third Listening with Empathy class, we're focusing on how you can stay bright and friendly when you actually start talking business with your client or customer. Let's walk through an everyday business encounter and experience this process in action.

Imagine that you've prepared yourself for the encounter and used several focus phrases to keep yourself grounded and friendly during the moment of encounter. You've chatted a bit – and now it's time to talk business. As you make sure to stay aware of your breathing throughout, also hold clearly in your mind the thought "I want to listen to this person's needs, and help satisfy those needs." Memorize this statement of intent so that it's in the back of your mind – and act on it by giving the person your full attention as you listen to their needs.

Naturally, part of your work involves presentation, intellectual planning, and mental focusing – but when relating with anyone, hold in mind that staying aware of your body in the present moment and giving yourself permission to feel good throughout are what actually make someone enjoy spending time with you. So, regularly say to yourself, "I'm here to enjoy this experience" or similar words so that you honor and respect yourself as well as your customer.

EMPATHIC COMMUNICATION

And, when the meeting is over, be sure to let go of all business focus and let the person know that you enjoyed spending time with them as a person – and that you genuinely look forward to seeing them again!

Please return to this training session a number of times until you learn it by heart and make it a natural part of all encounters!

Post-Encounter Processing

C H A P T E R   1 0

RECALL POSITIVE MOMENTS

If you're like most people, your life is busy and full with no time to spare. And, in your busy life you probably do what everyone else does – right after a business encounter, you move on to the next one. In this final section of this book, I want to strongly urge you to shift this busy pattern to include the essential final step in customer bonding and client loyalty.

I want to recommend that you create time and space when you're alone where you solidify in your own mind and heart your connection with the person you just met with – and project a clear desire and intent to meet with this person again.

This final solitary step in the Listening with Empathy method might seem the least important, but in reality it will prove equally important with the other three steps. If you don't pause to drop the customer experience into long-term memory and establish long-term future intent, you're actually damaging your future. Furthermore, if you don't grant yourself at least a few moments of reward time to feel good about the meeting and about yourself in general, you won't be bright and refreshed for the rest of the day. So, please make this fourth step in our Listening with Empathy process equally important to the first three. Finish the job right.

Your memory function remains a mysterious phenomenon in psychological research, but we do know that if you want to continue to hold someone in your mind, you must take short-term memory (which lingers in your mind right after an encounter) and remember that experience after the encounter in order to place it in your long-term memory banks. Often, you'll find that you recall a particular experience after it happens – and this establishes the experience as a long-term remembrance that you can access later, even 50 or more years later. But, if you fail to set an experience in long-term memory, the experience becomes very difficult or impossible to access.

YEARNING POWER

Yearning power is earning power. Reliving a moment in order to set that moment as a permanent memory does take time – not much, but a bit. And, because time is money, spending a bit of time remembering an encounter needs to be worthwhile in terms of your earning power. Let me take you a bit deeper into the earning power of yearning.

Yearning is usually defined as a strong need or wanting of what promises enjoyment, pleasure or fulfillment; a desire or longing.

In other words, when you yearn for something, you carry an intent, charge, desire, appetite, or hunger to attain that something. In this light, I've spent considerable time studying the phenomenon of appetite because, indeed, we are driven (often most wonderfully) by our hungers. Without them, we'd have no drive to eat wonderful meals, enjoy fantastic sex, travel the world and have adventures, settle into a cozy home life, or . . . get together with a client again.

Yearning is an active charge of intent in our energetic system that pushes us in a particular direction and broadcasts to the world our driving needs. I mentioned before that the Princeton Engineering Anomalies Research studies have now documented that the human mind does have the power to broadcast its need or desire or intent, and actually influence the functioning of a sensitive machine purely through this mysterious "yearning power" that we all possess.

Likewise, the Princeton studies proved that one mind can actively project a particular concept, image, or thought outward toward a specific human target, and that other person can receive and also respond to the concept or image being projected (please refer to www.princeton.edu/~pear).

When you put together your need to have a customer return to your company with your power to project this need toward them so that they actually experience your welcoming presence, you can begin to see the scientific dynamic. This is not New Age hocus-pocus I'm talking about here – it's cutting-edge science that is just beginning to explain the more subtle dimensions of empathy, as experienced from a distance.

Since ancient times, lovers have claimed that they can feel their dear one's presence at a distance, even halfway around the world. Now we have the scientific evidence showing that, indeed, this is not only possible but actually a universal, natural experience. The cognitive scientists and physicists will need a couple of new breakthroughs in order to explain the physical mechanics of the phenomenon the Princeton studies revealed – but we now know something very important is happening when we direct our yearning power toward a specific individual.

> Therefore, with this scientific background as our launching pad, I am recommending strongly that you pause after an encounter, and perhaps several times in the following days, to remember an enjoyable moment you spent with a customer and to project your intent (yearning) outward to this person so that they experience in their own heart and mind your friendly, welcoming presence.

You know how suddenly someone pops into your mind out of the blue? The Princeton studies strongly suggests that it's likely that that person was just thinking of you and thus triggered memories that you responded to. Imagine doing this with a customer – encouraging them to remember a positive moment in their meeting with you, which in turn triggers their desire to return to your establishment and be with you again.

This can all happen at mostly subliminal levels – but its effect can be the difference between the customer walking into your establishment again or not. That's the earning power of yearning.

DYNAMIC REFLECTION

How does the long-term memory process actually work in this regard? First of all, you must pause for a moment or two. You must tune into your breathing to quiet other thoughts and images, and focus your mind's attention back to the encounter you just had. You can do this right after the meeting if possible, or you can do it at lunch, while commuting home, while exercising, when taking a walk, or during formal reflection time in the evening. Just allow the memory to come to mind so that you experience in your heart the feelings of the moment.

Yearning is a feeling mixed with memories and imaginations. Memories can carry strong emotional components. And, it's the emotional dimension of the memory of the encounter that will prove most important to you. I've taught you how to make sure you have good feelings during an encounter of any kind. You can always find something enjoyable about a person, even if they're mostly a bother – that's your challenge and your power in bonding.

And, after the encounter you can return to the good feelings with this person and focus on these feelings rather than on the negative. That's the compassionate way to remember someone and to create a heart link with them that you can then project outward to encourage another business encounter.

Of course, there some people who are such a bother that you sincerely don't ever want to see them again. This is your right, and I encourage you to exercise it. You have your limits and your employer has no right to push you to violate those limits by spending future time with someone who was genuinely abusive to you. Write them off and move on.

But, with the majority of clients and customers, you'll be able to reap at least a few good moments from your encounter. Relive these moments; secure them in your long-term memory. Your focus of attention upon the short-term memory is the active power that creates long-term memory. And, your focus on your breathing and heart while you remember the experience is what activates the "feeling dimension" of the memory. So, yes, even here in post-encounter processing you'll be using your breath anchor to secure the important dimension of the memory.

ESTABLISHING THE LINK

Now we come to the true activation step. Again, even though it at first seems a bit far out, it isn't at all. It's the pragmatic act of establishing long-term contact with a customer. The act is sub-vocal, like the other focus phrases I'm teaching you. It stimulates your own intent to see this person again and broadcasts that intent to the other person.

As you hold the person in mind through reliving a positive memory from your encounter, you say silently to them from your heart, "Thank you for your visit. I hope to see you again soon!"

Bang – contact! It's like hitting the Enter key on your computer keyboard. You set up a clear line of communication based on a shared memory and a shared sense of heart contact. You create a bridge between the past, which is gone, and the present moment, which is always unfolding. You do this naturally with friends and lovers and family. Now you know the process, short and simple yet vital, for doing it with clients.

Practice this process if you like, right now. After reading this paragraph, put the book aside and remember a recent meeting or encounter you had with someone in any aspect of your day. Remember a positive moment you shared with them, perhaps a shared smile, a shared joke, or just the momentary pleasure of sharing space and time with them without talking at all – whatever the positive memory, focus on that experience with your breathing and your heart at the same time. Feel the positive experience you had with this person. And, silently say to them through the power of your own mind, "Thank you for your visit. I hope to see you again soon!"

PAUSE & EXPERIENCE

C H A P T E R   1 1

ESTABLISH FUTURE INTENT

As we near the end of this book, I'd like to take you a step further into the interplay of two seemingly opposite choices that you can make in furthering your career and financial success – the choice of being spontaneous or of acting out of future intent. I've been lauding both of these qualities separately. How do they interact and support each other rather than fight each other?

To answer this question we need to remember that the mind has several different functions. You're constantly choosing which functions to activate and which to temporarily put aside.

This is mind management at its essence – determining which mental hardware and software applications to engage at any moment in order to best meet the tasks and challenges at hand.

As I've explained in considerable detail in several books, you have five different modes of consciousness. First, there's your sensory and tactile present-moment awareness mode that directly connects your inner world and your physical body with the world around you. Second, there's your emotional mode, which enables you to respond to the world around you, express your feelings, and go into appropriate action. Your third consciousness mode is your ability to remember events that happened in the past and to project those memories as fantasies and imaginations of a possible future. Fourth, there's your cognitive thinking function for logically analyzing situations, reflecting with concepts about your past and future, and establishing conceptual and verbal intent regarding your future. And, finally, there's your integrative, intuitive, creative mental function, which brings everything together, sees the whole of a situation, and flashes with insights and great ideas.

You definitely need to maintain a healthy, active relationship with all five of these consciousness modes if you're going to succeed and enjoy a good life. But, most people are out of balance – they are either overly cognitive and lost in their own thoughts, or fixated on sensory stimulation, or caught up in the past and future, or stuck in intuitive mode and unable to focus and get a job done. If you look at your own tendencies, you'll find that a couple of the five consciousness modes dominate your daily awareness while others seem to fade into the background so you don't use them enough to your advantage.

Part of the Listening with Empathy process involves knowing how to shift from one mental mode to another in order to match the challenge of the moment with the appropriate mental mode.

I've been teaching you ways to exercise this "cognitive shifting" process. For instance, for when you're lost in thought, I've taught you how to shift actively into the perceptual mode of consciousness by focusing on the experience of your breathing and your whole-body participation in the present moment. I've shown you how to shift from cold, intellectual fixation to warm, heart-focused experience. And, I've shown you how to shift from a past-future, manipulative stance to present-moment spontaneity and intuitive participation.

All of these shifts are vital for waking up your empathic sense of positive engagement with customers and colleagues at work. There's another shift that I want to encourage you to also make, especially just before an encounter and right after an encounter – the establishment of clear intent. This mental act is definitely a temporary shift away from a quiet mind and spontaneous action toward a cognitive past-future function of the mind.

In the first section of this book, we talked about establishing clear intent regarding the immediate future and your coming encounter. Your intent in such business situations is to be friendly and spontaneous and to serve the person honestly through compassionate listening, and then take action to help satisfy the person's needs. Now in this fourth section of the book, I ask you, what is your intention and how can you best state it?

WHEN TO PUT YOURSELF FIRST

I've strongly advised that you put your customer or client first when actively engaged with them in person. This is the wise path to success at work because long-term customer loyalty is the key to success. But, if you never pause to put yourself and your needs first, you'll never establish your own clear intent in terms of your own needs.

Usually, the best time to put yourself first and state your personal needs and intent is during this reflective period of an encounter.

You've truly done your best to be of service to your client or customer or colleagues. You've fulfilled the empathy-first part of your bargain and done all you can to help others. Now, what about you?

You do have your own needs and yearnings and desires, and you do have a right to focus on making sure that you're fulfilling these personal needs. Many people go overboard with "service first" and end up denying their own needs – but this ultimately backfires because it's not really an honest stance to pretend that you're not interested in fulfilling your own needs. Honesty is absolutely essential for long-term success.

So, what are your needs? Why do you personally want to see that client who just walked out your door walk back in your door? Yes, you want to help that person fulfill their needs. And at the same time, you want that person to help fulfill your needs. We're living in a money-centric economy, so the honest truth is that you want to receive money from that person in exchange for equal goods and services. If you can't honestly fulfill their needs, you're honest and fair enough not to take their money without fulfilling their needs. But, otherwise, you do want that exchange to take place.

So, when you're alone in this fourth step of the process, be sure to pause and focus on your own needs and whether they're being met. Once you've established a long-term sense of contact and attraction with the person, give yourself a short break to reestablish your personal, driving intent.

"I WANT TO MAKE ENOUGH MONEY TO SATISFY MY OWN NEEDS."

Say it – do it! Be honest and upfront about your own needs and desires, and your intent to act to satisfy them even while you're being of service to others.

WHAT DO YOU NEED?

You probably have quite a few hungers, yearnings, passions, appetites, desires, and needs. You need to feel well loved and of value in the world. You need to keep yourself healthy. You need to have free time to just kick back and enjoy life. You need to feel you have power and choice and freedom in your society. You need to feel part of some sort of family, community, and larger human intent. And, you need to make enough money to have an enjoyable home and a reasonable amount of material possessions.

What other needs and desires, yearnings, and requirements

do you have that you feel you have a right to satisfy through making money and participating in your community? I encourage you right now to pause and take time to reflect on which of your needs are presently being satisfied, and which ones you still yearn or hunger to fulfill. Also, see how it feels in your throat, your heart, and your stomach to express out loud your personal-intent focus phrase a few times.

Put the book aside now if you want to, reflect on your needs, and memorize the focus phrase – then, say it to yourself as you stay aware of your breathing and your heart. Feel good in your heart as you state your own needs and personal intent.

"I want to make enough money to satisfy all of my own needs."

PAUSE & EXPERIENCE

SPONTANEOUS INTENT

When you regularly get honest with yourself and state your intent to make plenty of money in your work and satisfy your own needs, you will begin to establish this underlying intent as a primary one-liner that has a prominent place in your sense of identity and purpose. Then and only then will your spontaneous actions begin to merge with your intentions at a trustworthy level.

We discussed earlier that a lot of people don't trust their spontaneous selves because this trust often leads them away from their actual needs and intentions. This happens when you have personal needs and yearnings that are in conflict with your business intent.

> The underlying purpose of this book and all my training programs is to help you integrate the various needs and desires that drive you into a cohesive conscious sense of intent. Otherwise, you're going to continue sabotaging your conscious efforts through unconscious distortions of your intent.

This is why, over and over, we've explored how being of service to others is the optimal way to serve you - because what goes around does come around. Notice that the first step I recommend you make in preparation for a meeting is to make sure that you shift into feeling good inside your own skin. This is a need that will surely sabotage your business efforts if not placed front and center. We all want to feel good. If we don't feel good at work, we're going to rebel!

Because feeling good happens only when you're focused on your body in the present moment, I've also been training you to regularly shift into the present moment and to let go of the torture chamber realms of regretting the past and worrying about the future. So, in each preparation for an encounter you're making sure that you're taking care of those primary needs to feel good. Otherwise, as soon as you shift into

POST-ENCOUNTER PROCESSING

spontaneous relating with a customer, your inner child is going to take the opportunity to try to find some way to have fun – and often that will be quite counterproductive to your business intent.

If you're grounded in the present moment and feeling good in your breathing and your heart when you begin an encounter at work (or anyplace else), then you can set yourself free and relate spontaneously with your customer. You'll also have the inner trust that as you enjoy the present moment with this person, bond with them, and fulfill their needs, your spontaneous actions will remain in harmony with your personal intent to participate in a successful business interaction.

Learning to develop and trust your sense of spontaneous intent does take time. The programs in this book offer both quick advances you can make literally overnight and long-term methods that will steadily expand your ability to turn your work situation into a fulfilling, balanced, enjoyable, and profitable experience.

At the end of this book I'll present the Listening with Empathy program to you in one cohesive training process so that you can, over and over, move through the four-step system and get better and better at it. Every day will open up to you as an opportunity to feel even better at work, and to succeed at even higher levels even while you make new friends and satisfy your customers.

C H A P T E R 1 2

ENJOY TRUE SUCCESS

There's a final step I recommend for the end of a business encounter. This step goes beyond all business and survival needs and activities, especially if you have more than one sales, service, or team encounter a day. Be sure that at the end of the fourth step of the encounter process you pause just long enough to take a good, deep, non-business breath or two and step entirely out of your work identity. At least a few times a day, put aside your need to push toward success and financial well-being, and relish your success in playing the business game while keeping your greater identity alive and well.

I mention this because a special sense of personal power and pleasure emerges right at the moment you set aside all intent and forward business movement and remember that you are more than this role you're playing. You could have taken another, quite different path in life, and right at this moment you could be doing any number of other types of work to sustain yourself and your loved ones. You're playing this particular role just because that's how fate came to pass in your life. You are more than your job definition.

And, that greater self that you possess, that broader potential that isn't being tapped in your job definition, begins to suffocate if you don't regularly give it air space and acknowledgement.

This is especially important when meeting with clients because your capacity for heart-to-heart contact with them is not grounded in your job identity. Person-to-person engagement emerges from your sense of being a whole human being with a wide, interesting, and often heartwarming range of emotions, beliefs, and behaviors that extend beyond your job definition – if you let them.

There is a fine balance to be maintained between playing the role that gets your job done and satisfies the customer's specific needs, and revealing yourself beyond your business role so that you can share genuine contact with the person you're meeting with. You must adapt that balance to suit your particular personality and your business role. But, always be conscious of the balance – learn to let your personal light shine as much as possible, without distracting from the work at hand.

EMBRACE THE PLEASURE PRINCIPLE

We started this book by pointing out that customers enjoy employees who are enjoying themselves in their work. The entire drive of this book's discussion has centered on the need for you, as an employee at any level in your company, to manage your moods so that you broadcast a relaxed, interested, friendly presence.

Let's end this book by admitting up front that business does run on the pleasure principle, just as our basic personal drives lean away from pain and toward pleasure.

Even at the level of single-celled organisms that have been surviving on this planet for almost a billion years, the basic survival function that all beings share is that we have an instinctive, even reflexive, tendency to shy away from pain and toward pleasure. Pain, by definition, is an indicator that something is wrong and that we need to go into action to stave off damage or death. Pleasure, on the other hand, is an indicator that everything is okay, that we're doing quite well for the moment, and that we can relax a bit and enjoy the pure beingness of life.

Both pain and pleasure have their role in our lives, alerting us to dangers and the need for change and letting us know when we can ease up and rest assured that all is okay in our lives.

But, human beings in particular have distorted and even taken serious advantage of our ancient pain-pleasure programming. For instance, almost all commerce on the planet has fallen under the pull of mass media advertising where we are manipulated psychologically into believing that particular brands of products will make us feel better and relieve our negative condition – whereas this usually is not the case at all.

We also have developed attitudes based mostly on fear and greed that drive us into chronic stress states and to overwork when we could ease up and enjoy life more. One of the truly sad statistics of our time is that we're working more and more and more – and not really getting more and more and more pleasure and fulfillment out of it. Our anxieties drive us to torture our minds and bodies with too much stressful work and not enough relaxed play – and the result is that far too many people at work are in negative moods and at low energy levels, and not at all enjoyable to relate with.

You'll remember that I stated the employee's bill of rights earlier in this book. The hopeful element of that discussion was that it now makes perfect business sense for executives and managers to focus on making sure that their employees are enjoying themselves at work – because when employees are happy and having a good time, customers enjoy the emotional atmosphere of the company and want to return for more business and enjoyment.

Therefore, company policy needs to be solidly grounded on the pleasure principle – not only for employees but for high-end management as well. Every rotten mood apple has the potential to ruin the entire barrel.

DEMAND YOUR PLEASURE AT WORK

And so we return to the beginning of our discussion and your need, first and foremost, to say often to yourself, "I give myself permission to feel good at work." How does this statement translate into actual experience on the job? "Feeling good" can be encouraged on numerous dimensions, all of which your employer should be consciously enhancing.

1. Enjoyable physical sensations: This translates to freedom to move, stretch, and yawn regularly; to enjoy adequately comfortable chairs; etc.

2. Pleasant sights and sounds: This refers to a working environment that's esthetically pleasing. (You'll note that the audio programs on my website at www.listeningwith empathy.com offer a most beautiful collage of nature photographs to enjoy and to help augment a sense of natural beauty at work.)

3. Freedom to stay aware of your breathing: Do this to maintain contact with the present moment and to enjoy your second-to-second experience of the present moment.

4. Enjoyment of warm, heart-centered emotions: These emotions emerge when you quiet bothersome worries and make genuine contact with co-workers and customers.

5. An overall sense that you are successful at work: This

means that you feel you're receiving a fair wage for your work, that your job is challenging, that there is an opportunity for advancement, and that you are recognized for your good work.

6. Assurance that your work won't be too stressful: You want to be able to enjoy your job and not be damaged through mental or emotional stressors that hurt your health and relationships.

7. The sense of being on a winning team: You should feel secure and confident that your company will succeed and that you will have a reasonably low-risk future.

I'm sure you can identify other pleasure-first dimensions, but this list provides the general idea. There's nothing on this list that in the long run will reduce productivity; just the opposite, as more and more studies indicate that a bright, happy, healthy workforce is one of the surest indicators of high production. So, you can work with your employer to optimize the pleasure principle at work. The very notion sounds anti-business, but the logic bears out the intent.

And, every time you end a meeting or engagement of any kind at work, see if you can shift into the fourth step of post-encounter processing and reflection, where you not only re-establish long-term memory and heart contact with the person you met with, but where you also reset your primary intent and give yourself a bit of free breathing space in the bargain. Start and end your day with clear intent: "I give myself permission to feel good!"

PROGRAM REVIEW

POST-ENCOUNTER PROCESSING

Quick Review

This fourth phase involves pausing to reflect on a recent sales or service encounter and deciding purposefully how to follow up. It's so important to take time to re-experience positive aspects of the encounter and focus on your genuine desire to meet again with this person. Please develop the strong habit of always pausing for this reflective step.

Key Focus Phrases

"Thank you for your visit."

"I hope to see you again!"

"I want enough money to satisfy my needs and live well."

"I give myself permission to feel good at work."

Points to Remember

All too often, we move from one encounter to the next – especially if we're in retail sales but also in the office – without pausing to move through the essential fourth phase of a successful encounter. Failing to move through the reflection/processing phase of a meeting can seriously limit the long-term success of that meeting.

- Recall positive moments: If you are practicing what you've learned in this book, during each new encounter you'll have quite enjoyable moments (even if the person you met with was a bit of a bother). You can choose to enjoy the experience – and then it's vital to pause afterward and remember those good feelings, to establish long-term memory, and to make solid, lasting heart contact with the person you met with.

- Visualize your future intent: This book is all about customer loyalty, which means return visits to your establishment. Based on the evidence from PEAR that your thought and intent carry genuine power, after each meeting you will want to pause and establish in your mind the clear intent to meet again with your customer or client.

- Enjoy your own success: The final part of a successful meeting (one in which you did your best to serve your customer) is the act of pausing long enough to enjoy your feeling of doing good and succeeding at work. Breathe in your good feelings, acknowledge your own prowess, and enjoy satisfaction in what you do – that's your inherent human right!

Reflection Time

For every experience you have, it's important to devote time to the reflection process of the mind, where you contemplate what has happened and gain an expanded understanding of who you are and what you're doing. This is especially important at work. Here are questions to ask yourself after each business encounter.

A. Were you able to stay aware of your breathing and whole-body presence during your meeting? What actually happened inside your mind and awareness during the meeting? What might you do to stay more aware, relaxed, and friendly during a meeting?

B. Are you becoming a good listener who gives all of your attention to the customer without interfering with their expression of their needs? Can you watch your breathing, stay tuned into your heart, and listen with your full attention all at the same time?

C. Is it easy to remember positive experiences that you had with a client or customer? Do you like taking the time to reflect and remember? Can you visualize the person you just met without any judgmental thoughts?

D. How does it feel to state your intent of wanting to meet with a customer again – are you getting good at broadcasting your intent of win-win success and enduring friendship?

E. Do you regularly pause to acknowledge and enjoy your own success? Do you regularly state your intent not only to serve others, but also to make enough money to satisfy your own needs?

Exercise: Post-Encounter Processing

Memorizing a step-by-step procedure is the best way to move through the post-encounter processing phase of a successful encounter. Here's a simple exercise you can follow after each business meeting. You can move through this in just one minute if that's all the time you have. Hopefully your employer will begin to recommend that you take a few minutes, if possible, for processing – everyone benefits!

1. Pause, tune into your breathing . . . give yourself a little free time for reflection – and remember positive moments that spring to mind, of being together with your customer or client. And, say to yourself as if speaking to this person, "Thank you for your visit!"

2. Shift from the recent past to your future intent of seeing this person and doing business with them again. Say to them in your mind, "I hope to see you again."

3. Focus for at least a few breaths on recent memories when you did your job well. Reinforce in your mind your intent to succeed at work by saying to yourself, "I intend to make enough money to live well."

4. End your reflection by saying to yourself, "I give myself permission to feel good at work." Let these words carry you positively into whatever you do next!

AUDIO SCRIPT: CLASS FOUR

Go to www.listeningwithempathy.com for audio guidance.

Pausing after a business encounter to reflect on the experience and to set your intent to meet with that person again is often the hardest to remember to do. Here's a guided process to help you effortlessly move through the steps of post-encounter processing.

First of all . . . make the act of setting aside a bit of time so that there's enough breathing room to move through the process . . . tune into your breathing . . . the feelings in your heart . . . your entire body right here, right now . . . and allow positive memories to come to mind of the person you just met with . . . remember feeling good during the meeting . . . and let the good memories of this person take root within you.

Secondly . . . shift from the past to the future and let yourself feel in your heart your intent to meet with this person, and enjoy sharing space and time with them again . . . Say to them in your mind, "I hope to see you again sometime!" and feel your positive heart-to-heart connection.

Thirdly . . . As you breathe into these good feelings of being connected with your customer and anticipating doing business with them again, acknowledge your own good work and your business intent by saying, "I want to make enough money to live well."

And finally . . . end your short reflection break by saying to yourself, "I give myself permission to feel good at work" and go on with your day with your focus on your breathing and good feelings in your heart!

FINAL WORDS

SPREADING BRIGHTNESS AT WORK

We've now covered about ten thousand miles of research and methodology in about 200 pages – thanks for sticking with me. I hope you'll use each section of this book not just as a read-once process, but as a long-term manual for everyday guidance. This process does take time to master, even though you'll feel positive benefits in the very first week.

What have we covered? Here's the format of our four-part method that I laid out for you in the beginning, which we've now moved through step by step. Notice how you respond to these same words now that you've learned what's behind them. And, note to what extent you feel that you've learned the method being talked about and to what extent you now need to discipline yourself over the next weeks to truly make this Listening with Empathy process your own.

- Phase 1 – Preparation: Before meeting with a customer or client, it's vital to put aside any stress, worries, or judgments that might pollute the encounter – and shift your focus toward positive feelings and heart-centered emotions.

- Phase 2 – The Moment of Encounter: Right when you

meet someone, present an honest, friendly, non-judgmental greeting, and offer relaxed space. New techniques can help you maintain a bright inner center, present a friendly presence, and converse with relaxed spontaneity, acceptance, and enjoyment.

- Phase 3 – Empathic Communication: When you begin talking business, maintain clear intent to be of service and enable your customer to truly satisfy their needs. By encouraging an enjoyable emotional atmosphere, you can make sure the customer feels in good hands and well taken care of.

- Phase 4 – Processing: This fourth phase involves pausing to reflect on a recent sales or service encounter and deciding purposefully how to follow up. You'll learn to re-experience positive aspects of the encounter and focus on your desire to meet with this person again.

That's the sum of this method – four steps for you to master. And what should you do now that you've finished your first read of this book? I recommend two steps:

- Step one: Continue to use this book as a training manual, re-reading each chapter and working with the specific learning programs in the back of this book – they are there for daily guidance through the learning process. After each section of the book, as you saw, there's a quick reference summary of the section and full guidance through the process. Return to these summaries often! If you want, you can go to www. listeningwithempathy.com and take advantage of the audio training there. Let my voice guide you through the four-step process over and over so that you truly internalize the process and make it your own. This will take three weeks of the daily program, requiring just ten minutes a day, to accomplish.

- Step two: Each day at work, take the focus phrase you're learning that day with you to work and exercise using the process you've learned thus far with each new customer or client. Really integrate this method into your permanent work life. This program will work only to the extent that you discipline yourself to practice and apply the four steps regularly at work. I've done my part; the entire learning process is awaiting you. Now it's your personal challenge to employ just a bit of daily discipline. Turn to the guided exercises at the end of each section of this book, and the final summary following these words. Also, use the full audio training at www.listeningwith empathy.com – and make sure, every day, to expand your mastery of the process.

The good news is that every day each new step will make you feel better. Yes, I've built this entire learning system on the pleasure principle – why not! So, approach the learning experience eagerly and with the intent of having fun and feeling good for the ten minutes you are in training. At the same time, dig in and really master this so that the focus phrases come naturally to mind often when you're at work and serve as a launchpad into brighter, more empathic and enjoyable encounters with everyone you meet at work – and at home, too!

Thanks for your focus and attention throughout this book. I look forward to your online presence as well. We're expanding a long-term community where you can get all the support you need in every aspect of your day. The intent of the book and the website throughout is to make sure that you learn this method by heart and make it a natural new part of your business success. Enjoy!

PROGRAM REVIEW

PHASE 1: PREPARING FOR AN ENCOUNTER

A. Two-Minute Preparation

1. Say to yourself, "I feel the air flowing in and out of my nose . . ."

   . . . and as you inhale, tune in fully to this sensory experience.

2. Say to yourself, "I also feel the movements in my chest and belly. . ."

   . . . and expand your awareness to include your whole body.

3. Say to yourself, "I'm aware of the feelings in my heart . . ."

   . . . and breathe into the feelings you find in your heart.

4. Say to yourself, "I give myself permission to feel good . . ."

   . . . and tune into any good feelings you find inside.

5. Say to yourself, "My mind is quiet, my emotions calm . . ."

   . . . and enjoy the feeling of inner calm in your mind.

6. Say to yourself, "I honor and respect the person I'm meeting with . . ."
. . . and let acceptance fill your mind and open your heart.

7. Say to yourself, "I feel good toward my own self . . ."
. . . and experience the heart feelings these words awaken.

8. Say to yourself, "I'm ready to be friendly and cheerful, to listen without manipulation, and to help satisfy this person's needs . . ."
. . . and allow these words to resonate throughout your being.

B. Preparation: Short, Short

For when you have just a few moments, here's a special version of the preparation process to use:

1. Say to yourself, "I'm tuned into my breathing . . ."
. . . and turn your mind's attention to the air flowing in and out of your nose, and the movements in your chest and belly as you breathe.

2: Say to yourself, "I'm aware of the feelings in my heart . . ."
. . . and let your awareness expand and include whatever's happening in your heart . . . and welcome good feelings in your heart!

3: Say to yourself, "I let go of worries and feel peaceful inside . . ."

. . . and as the words impact your inner experience, breathe into an expansion of both confidence and pure pleasure.

4: Say "I'm ready to accept, to serve, and to succeed . . ."

. . . and let each of these key elicitor words . . . accept . . . serve . . . succeed . . . ground you in your primary intent in the coming meeting.

1. "I'm tuned into my breathing . . ."

2. "I'm aware of the feelings in my heart . . ."

3. "I let go of worries and feel peaceful inside . . ."

4. "I'm ready to accept, to serve, and to succeed . . ."

PHASE 2: THE MOMENT OF ENCOUNTER

1. Preparation: Preparation is certainly half the story of successfully encountering someone. Be sure to move through either the one- or two-minute

process you learned earlier – and also do your regular homework for enhancing your power to come from the heart and make genuine contact. Say to yourself, "I am here now – breathing freely."

2. Breath anchor: Right when you come face to face with someone, train yourself to hold your primary attention to your breathing – to the air flowing in and out, the movements in your chest and belly, and your ongoing feeling of groundedness. Say to yourself, "I feel grounded in my heart, pelvis, legs, and feet."

3. Sharing space: Expand your awareness to include the air around you – the space you're now sharing with this person. Let this shared medium bond the two of you and hold your attention in the present moment. Say to yourself, "I want to make a new friend."

4. Be spontaneous: Rather than acting from a planned script, just relax, give yourself permission to enjoy yourself, and let your body move spontaneously. Say to yourself, "I set myself free to feel good right now."

Practice mastering this process – give yourself time to play with this inner method and don't be upset if you slip into old habits. Just keep returning to the process and moving through it again and again.

PHASE 3: EMPATHIC COMMUNICATION

You want to make money when you're at work. You want to serve and sell and succeed. The question is how best to do that – and at the same time respect and honor both yourself and your client. You have learned in the first two sections of this method how to prepare for a positive interaction and stay heart-centered during the moment of encounter. Now you're set to do business feeling empathic and in service mode.

1. The secret lies in memorizing and holding in mind several focus phrases that enable you to remain aware of underlying qualities of heart and mind that keep you positive and compassionate while doing business. Primary among these focus phrases is "I want to listen to this person's needs."

2. After you have listened well and heard the person's needs, it's time to shift into being of service and determining if you can satisfy those needs.

Say to yourself, "I choose to help this person satisfy their needs." Hold this clear intent in the back of your mind while you're listening and talking to your customer. You'll feel good with this intent in your heart – and by feeling good and helpful, you'll encourage a win-win situation.

3. Throughout, rather than getting tense when advancing your business intent, hold the focus phrase "I'm here to enjoy this experience" in mind. Your customers will relax and enjoy your presence – and want to return to do business with you again!

PHASE 4: POST-ENCOUNTER PROCESSING

Memorizing a step-by-step procedure is the best way to move through the processing phase of a successful encounter. Here's a simple exercise you can follow after each business meeting. You can move through this in just one minute if that's all the time you have. Hopefully your employer will begin to recommend that you take a few minutes, if possible, for post-encounter processing – everyone benefits!

1. Pause, tune into your breathing . . . give yourself a little free time for reflection. Remember posi-

tive moments of being with your customer or client. And then, say to yourself as if speaking to this person, "Thank you for your visit!"

2. Shift from the recent past to your future intent of seeing this person and doing business with them again. Say to them in your mind, "I hope to see you again."

3. Focus for at least a few breaths on recent memories when you did your job well. Reinforce in your mind your intent to succeed at work by saying to yourself, "I want to make enough money to live well."

4. End your reflection by saying to yourself, "I give myself permission to feel good at work." Let these words carry you positively into whatever you do next!

DAILY EMPATHY-BOOST WORKOUT
(3–5 M I N U T E S)

(Also available online as audio guidance online)

Each day, right when you get up, when you are commuting to work, or during a few minutes at work, you'll benefit greatly if you prep your mind and emotions by moving through the following inner process. You can also use our online audio guidance for effortless shifting into optimum empathic mode.

Just make yourself comfortable however feels best right now . . . stretch a bit if that feels good . . . yawn perhaps . . . and tune into your breathing . . . the air flowing in and out of your nose . . . the movements in your chest and belly as you breathe . . . and expand your awareness to also include the feelings in your heart right now . . . accept them . . . and say to yourself, "I give myself permission to feel good."

As you give your full attention to your breathing . . . your heart . . . your whole-body presence . . . your mind becomes quiet . . . you can let go of worries and other mental bothers . . . and fully enjoy the pure pleasure of just being alive right now . . . breathing . . . accepting the world just as it is . . . and being ready to enjoy your new day.

You have the choice of feeling bad or feeling good in your

own heart today . . . just say to yourself, "I choose to feel good and be friendly with everyone I meet."

And, as you just relax now and enjoy the breaths coming . . . and going . . . without any effort at all . . . open up and let acceptance and love come flowing into your heart . . . let yourself build up a good feeling charge of empathy in your heart . . . in your entire body . . . say to yourself again, "I give myself permission to feel good at work!"

And now, focus a bit on your intent to both serve your customers and clients, and also to succeed at your job and make plenty of money so you can live a good life . . . say to yourself, "I am here to serve, to flourish, and to enjoy life."

And, as you move into your workday, you can hold this good charge of empathy in your heart and mind . . . and remember to hold your favorite focus phrases in mind throughout the day . . . as you stay focused in your breathing . . . your heart . . . your enjoyable whole-body presence . . . this day is your day!

Enjoy!

FOCUS PHRASES – AT A GLANCE

Phase 1

"I am here now – breathing freely . . ."

"I'm aware of the feelings in my heart . . ."

"My mind is quiet, my emotions calm . . ."

"I honor and respect the person I'm meeting with . . ."

Phase 2

"I feel good toward my own self . . ."

"I feel grounded in my heart, pelvis, legs, and feet . . ."

"I want to make a new friend . . ."

"I am here to serve, flourish, and enjoy myself . . ."

Phase 3

"I want to listen to this person's needs . . ."

"I want to help this person satisfy their needs . . ."

"I want us both to win today . . ."

"I choose to enjoy this business encounter . . ."

Phase 4

"Thank you for your visit."

"I hope to see you again!"

"I deserve enough money to live well."

"I give myself permission to feel good at work."

ONLINE TRAINING AND SUPPORT

This book contains all of the information and instruction you will need to fully succeed with the Listening with Empathy program. However, we've found that many people also value audio guidance and instruction when mastering a method such as this one. The freedom to close your eyes and listen to your teacher guiding you through an inner process can make the learning experience even more enjoyable.

Therefore, to supplement the learning power of this book you will find online at www.listeningwithempathy.com a full set of streaming audio programs to further assist you in the learning process. These audio programs are short and can be listened to either at home, while commuting, at work – or anywhere! Simply upload the programs to your mp3 player. You'll also find a number of related training programs for other aspects of your work and home life, and an online community of others learning to apply these basic principles and methods to augment their success and fulfillment. My aim throughout is to serve you well!

www.listeningwithempathy.com

CORPORATE PROGRAMS

The Listening with Empathy method taught in this book, online, and at live training presentations is part of our larger Take Charge at Work executive- and employee-training program delivered via print, DVD, and online, and via live presentations, instruction, and support. Awareness management is, without question, a highly valuable, new dimension in optimizing your company's performance, profit, and long-term sustainability. Our corporate programs enable you to obtain this training fast and economically through a three-tier training system. Please click the Corporate Programs button at www.listeningwithempathy.com for further information.

ABOUT THE AUTHOR

John Selby is a psychologist, cognitive science researcher, entrepreneur, and international speaker with 30 years experience developing these core mind-management techniques. He conducted groundbreaking cognitive research at the National Institutes of Health and the Bureau of Research in Neurology and Psychiatry and the New Jersey Neuro-Psychiatric Institute. Founder and former CEO of The BrightMind Network and currently head of Consciousness Management Systems, John is a specialist in creating online experiential instruction formats that deliver effective and affordable training to organizations throughout the world.

Selby is an engaging speaker who has led many seminars on topics related to consciousness management. He has appeared widely on national television and radio.

www.johnselby.com

Hampton Roads Publishing Company

. . . for the evolving human spirit

HAMPTON ROADS PUBLISHING COMPANY publishes books on a variety of subjects, including metaphysics, spirituality, health, visionary fiction, and other related topics.

For a copy of our latest trade catalog, call toll-free, 800-766-8009, or send your name and address to:

HAMPTON ROADS PUBLISHING COMPANY, INC.
1125 STONEY RIDGE ROAD • CHARLOTTESVILLE, VA 22902
e-mail: hrpc@hrpub.com • www.hrpub.com